Sheepdog Training

an
ALL-BREED APPROACH

Sheepdog Training

an
ALL-BREED APPROACH

Mari Taggart

△lpine Publications
P.O. Box 7027 • Loveland, CO 80537

Library of Congress Cataloging in Publication Data

Taggart, Mari
  Sheepdog training : an all-breed approach / Mari Taggart. 2nd ed.
      p.   cm.
  Includes bibliographical references
  ISBN 0-931866-50-2
  1. Sheep dogs—Training.   I. Title.
  SF428.6.T34   1991
  636.7'3—dc2O   90-19715
                                                            CIP

Second Edition 1991
First Edition 1986

ISBN 0-931866-50-2

Printed in the United States of America.

Credits
Cover design: Joan Harris
Cover Photos: (Top) Keelain's Kid Kaila, C.D., ATD, and STD, owned by Kay Lorrain. (Bottom) Geier's Sweet Cindy Lou owned by Grisila Geier. Photo by Augusta Farley.

Contents

DEDICATION

To the special dogs
that have so greatly enriched
my life over the years—
MOSS ROGUE
whose love, devotion and ability to teach
me all he knew were forever special;
JETEYE ALICE
For taking me down a peg
when I thought I knew it all;
SPECKLES and TWEED
for showing me that
canine hope and strength of character
can sometimes surpass that of humans.

It has been a privilege to know them.

INTRODUCTION

For the last several years I have been teaching all-breed herding classes and seminars in the western United States. During that time I have had the privilege of working with a wide variety of breeds and their owners. There is a greater interest than ever before in sheep-dog training—among ranchers and farmers and also among those who want to learn to train their dog to herd livestock as a hobby.

There are any number of training books written by Border Collie owners for Border Collie owners; many are very good books. But to someone with a breed other than Border Collies, or to someone whose dog just doesn't fit the "perfect" mold so often described in these books, these well-written books may provide very little help at all. The vast majority of Border Collie books deal with rather advanced training; much is taken for granted. This is not what the novice needs. In this book, I've tried to present an approach that can be used with a variety of breeds and that takes nothing for granted on the part of the reader. We will start from the "ground up" as they say. This does not mean that we will ignore or disparage Border Collie train-ing or trainers. I happen to be one of them, and there is no doubt that the British with their 300 years of expert training can really show us a great deal—it would be foolish to ignore the great discoveries they have made. Yet, for those with European breeds, American breeds, or even those "other" British breeds, the advice cannot always be taken literally. In order to train all breeds you must remain flexible and adaptive.

Almost any dog with a "gathering style" can be trained with

this book. It is not written for natural driving dogs. I have rarely seen any natural driving dogs except among Australian Cattle Dogs, and this book is not intended for training them, unless you have one with a natural gathering style. Almost any trainer should be able to read and understand these methods and, I hope, go out and apply them with their own dog! Though it is not intended as a book for training trial dogs, it is possible to use a dog trained by these techniques to compete successfully in trials. You are only limited by your time and determination, and your dog by its natural abilities. Trials are not just Border Collie territory anymore. Many of the trials are now all-breed events.

Though I admit to having my favorites, I have learned through experience to have a very healthy admiration for many breeds and I have learned to not rely on stereotypes, for as soon as you do, along comes a dog to make you feel ridiculous. A good herding dog is a joy to own, be it tall or short, shaggy or smooth-haired, noisy or quiet, and MANY breeds can do the job.

It is my hope that this book will bring joy into your life through one of life's most precious treasures—a faithful sheepdog.

ACKNOWLEDGEMENT

There are really two schools of thought in training sheepdogs. One states that you work with what nature (and wise breeders) has inherently put in the dog. The other school says that the trainer must make the dog a robot of his master's will.

I was fortunate enough, early on in my training experience, to meet and work with men whose lives had been devoted to the training and handling of good sheepdogs, who recognized the truth of the idea that one does not breed supernatural workers only to make them robots. The saying "Wait on Nature," is an old one, and says a lot about the better ways of sheepdog training.

I want to publicly thank a few of those men who gave of their time and talents to help a struggling novice—I will forever be grateful to them for their patience and great examples. The first is Arthur Allen, who taught me by example the concepts of great sportsmanship, humility and gratitude for dogs, as well as for his brilliant training ideas. Les Bruhn (who I'm sure I gave many an anxious moment), coached me in the finer points of handling and helped me so much in the beginning. Reg Griffon taught me that training is a lifetime commitment, and also taught me more about handling sheep than anyone I've ever met. To them, and many others, thank you for bringing great joy to my life.

Work in an area large enough for the dog to feel a sense of accomplishment in moving the stock.

1
Getting Started

To begin herding training all you really need is yourself, your dog and something to herd—ducks, sheep, goats or calves. The primary goal is to teach your dog to move stock efficiently, calmly and quietly from one point to another. It is important to never lose sight of the fact that livestock have feelings, they are valuable, and they must not be treated too roughly at any time. There may be times when your dog may need to take a nip at a sheep to defend himself, or heel a calf that refuses to move, but any unnecessary roughness should be discouraged. As you begin the training, remember that your stock will get tired or frightened at times. Be humane to them. Never allow your dog to harm the stock "just to build interest."

A herding dog is a *catalyst for movement*. That is, his instinct and his function is to move livestock in a predetermined direction. In the case of the gathering (fetching) dog (the kind this book is written for), your dog's goal will be to bring the stock toward you. At first this will be a very crude attempt, but as the dog learns to take time and feels more confident, his gather will become more refined and efficient.

All of the British breeds with the exceptions of the Old English Sheepdog and some Corgis are gathering, or fetching dogs. Of the Australian breeds, only the Australian Cattle Dog does not gather, and there is a small percentage of this breed that gathers. Of the American breeds, the Catahoula Leopard is a gathering (circling) breed, and a large percentage of the Australian Shepherd and English Shepherd are natural gathering dogs. Of the European and Middle Eastern herding breeds, all are gathering dogs, with the exception of a small percentage of Bouviers. So you see that gathering (fetching) is practiced by most of the world's herding dogs. Although they are not always used for this purpose, the gathering instinct provides the foundation for their herding desire.

Often I am asked, "How long will it take me to really get a good start on my dog?" For a novice, I usually estimate about six months, if you work regularly, three times a week or more. A professional can turn out a pretty good started dog in about two months, but they *are* professional, and they probably train twice a day in short sessions. Have patience and learn the lessons thoroughly. We Americans, especially, always want everything right away. There is no Mac-Donalds fast food of sheep dog training. We need to learn how the dog works, how he thinks, and how to become good trainers who can train more than one type of dog. Fifteen years ago an old, very wise sheepdog trainer told me that learning to train sheepdogs was something that would take a lifetime—I might add a lifetime of tremendous fun and challenge. There just are no shortcuts. Now that I've been at it for fifteen years, and have had some success, I never forget that I am still learning and growing as a trainer. A lifetime commitment to training may sound scary to you. If so, just take one day

It is essential that you work a large enough flock to teach the dog its directions. A minimum of three, and up to fifty, head is good. Pictured is Dixie Von Shafferhaus, German Shepherd, with David Shaffer.

at a time and you will enjoy it more than any other hobby. One day you may look back and see how far you've come and want to go farther still!

One last thing—if you get the chance to work with a top rate Border Collie trainer, jump at the chance. This book is not meant to replace personal instruction. Seeing a dog and trainer in action is easier than trying to picture a technique from a written description. Be very selective, however, of any instructor you pick. There are instant experts in this field who have done shocking damage to beginning dogs that some dogs never get over. Stick to established Border Collie trainers. They have the vast experience those in other breeds just don't have. It's hard to argue with 80 years or more of experience. There are also some good younger Border Collie trainers who have made quite a mark in trials and who train other handlers for trials. In some breeds, the "instant expert" syndrome is very prevalent. Beware!

Decide on a personal goal for your training and stick to it, whether it is to have fun or to learn enough to enter trials. Each day, break your goals down to something manageable. Always remember that YOU are the teacher and your dog is the pupil. Plan to do lessons each time you work. For example, your goal one day might be "today I am going to teach Rover to lift sheep off the fence toward me in the proper way," or "today I am going to teach Rover to establish a smoother, straighter approach to the stock." I had a very sweet gal in one of my classes and when I asked her what her goal was she replied, "I want this dog to work!" While this is certainly a noble goal, try not to be this "cosmic" in your thinking; narrow it down so that you will be able to take each lesson one step at a time.

UNDERSTANDING THE HERDING INSTINCT

To fully understand the herding instinct we must go back to the origin of the dog's relationship with human beings. I have read that the dog's desire to herd animals comes from an innate "humanlike love" that the dogs have for the livestock. Nothing could be farther from the truth. People who believe that their dog herds because of its great love for sheep are always shocked and frightened the first time their dog makes a dive for a sheep to bite it.

The most commonly accepted theory is that a doglike animal first became man's friend through becoming a scavenger of the offal from his kills. Then, gradually, the dog participated in the hunt, and man saw that the dog's help made things easier. Since these dogs hunted on their own, hunting with man (another pack member to them) was an easy transition. It was likely that the faster dogs would outrun the hunted animals, circling in front of them to slow them down or turn them back so that man could kill them.

We can stop right here as far as herding instinct is concerned, for this is what has formed the (albeit crude) basis for today's herding instinct. Modern day wolves demonstrate the ability of some pack members to outrun and "head" moose and caribou, while the slower pack members bring up the rear and either try to bring down the prey by slashing at its body and legs, or wait for the heading wolves to turn the prey back to them.

From earliest records we know that when man domesticated livestock, the dog had already become a part of the human world. The Bible mentions "dogs of the flock" and there is no doubt that some of these dogs were huge, savage brutes whose job was to drive off predators. But others, smaller in build, were kept for herding purposes, and the first evidences of selective breeding for herding traits are seen. There were dogs for hunting, dogs for war, dogs for guarding and dogs for herding (some dogs did "double duty," herding by day and guarding by night.)

It is always wise to remember, however, that the origin of the herding instinct is the dog's instinct to hunt. His desire to work with you while doing so derives from his pack instinct. The livestock, also, respond to centuries-old instincts when they were prey and were hunted by doglike animals. Thus a flock of 100 sheep (which, if they decided to fight, could easily trample one dog to death) will freely move away from the one dog who approaches them. The manner in which they respond is often dependent on the dog's attitude and posture. Sheep learn to ignore a big, white Komondor, who looks just like a sheep and acts more like one than a dog, but move fearfully from a Border Collie, whose black and white color, stalking approach and intensity make them recall those predator/prey days.

Most young dogs at some point will try to bite stock they shouldn't and must learn through training that this is not acceptable. But it should not come as a shock to you that your dog may try this, all the more so if you reach for an animal to catch it. This surely awakens those memories of when the dog helped man catch and kill prey. So be prepared—this is natural—but do not tolerate it just the same. The beauty of the dog is that training overcomes instinctive urges (we teach a dog not to fight with every other dog that comes on his property, or to ignore bitches in season in the show ring, or to come even if he's hot in pursuit after a rabbit.)

I have owned dogs who gave every impression of caring for their stock, much as human parents care for their children. But I do not feel that this was instinctive on the dog's part—more likely it was a product of training (which had modified the dog's instinct to bite) and conditioning. I have also seen highly trained sheepdog trial winners take part in killing ducks in the company of a pack of predatory dogs. Shepherds throughout history have believed *any* dog, even the best sheepdogs, will kill livestock, *given the right circumstances*.

A well-bred herding dog is a dog from lineage where certain traits have been selected over others. A naturally predatory dog (one that is impossible to train *not* to be predatory) rarely gets bred from in the herding world, so it is easy to control any predatory behavior while working most well-bred herding dogs.

Ellen Roja and Winn at Cummington, Mass. Sheepdog Trial. Photo by Carole L. Presberg.

A Bearded Collie working.

2

Selecting a Herding Dog

ABOUT THE DIFFERENT BREEDS

There are a good many breeds of dogs that make superior herding dogs. Following are a few comments about the herding breeds I've worked with, but remember, these are only generalities, and your dog may not be quite like the ones I've helped train. If your dog needs special work, by all means be flexible and willing to adopt new ideas.

The Australian Cattle Dog

Some Cattle Dogs are natural gathering dogs and should be started on goats or young calves that are easy to turn. These are strong, aggressive workers that may occasionally require a stern correction to get a point across. Much depends on their relationship with their trainer.

The Australian Kelpie

The slick-coated Australian import with much natural talent, Kelpies are bred in their native land for varied duties, many lines specializing in certain tasks such as trial dog or paddock dog. Be sure the one you get is bred to do what you want him to do. They are fairly biddable, with a gathering style, but occasionally can be strong willed and a few don't like commanding at all.

(Upper Left) **Ch. Parcana Portrait, H.C., R.O.M.,** owned by Mrs. Richard Parker, a proven producer of working Beardies.

(Upper Right) **W.C.C. (1979) Working Champion Jet Eye Alice, C.D.,** with her award from the W.C.C. Alice is an Australian Cattle Dog, owned by the author.

(Left) **Imp. Bullenbong Bulli CDX,** an Australian Kelpie owned by Gail Ross.

(Below) **ASCH Apache Tears of Timberline, U.D., A.T.D.,** an Australian Shepherd owned by Nick Davis.

The Australian Shepherd

This breed does not have any one herding style, so both driving and gathering dogs (and some that have no style or ability) may be found within this breed. They range from very, very good to just awful. The solution is to get a well-bred Aussie from parents who work the way you want your pup to work, and don't settle for less. A good Aussie is very trainable and eager, and, with a committed trainer, can do just about anything.

The Bearded Collie

Another of my favorites. Many make exceptional herders, and of this breed there are two types, the huntaway and the ones with eye. The huntaways bark constantly in their work, while the ones with eye are quiet, but both types gather. This breed is very biddable, and the hard part is to convince their owners of this fact—many of them spoil their dogs and refuse to believe the Beardie is anything more than a giant Lhasa Apso. This is a real shame since the Beardie is every bit as good as his close cousin, the Border Collie.

The Belgian Malinois

This rare breed seems different from its cousins, the Tervs and Sheepdogs. Few are in this country, and not many seem to have the instinct to really _herd_, perhaps due to their involvement as police dogs. However, this hasn't hampered the German Shepherd and others who have done police duty, so there seems no reason why the Malinois couldn't do the work.

The Belgian Tervuren and Belgian Sheepdog

I have grouped them together since their styles (and origins) are so close. All the better ones seem to fetch (gather) instinctively, and most are a bit aggressive at the start and must be taught control. They are highly biddable (easily trained) dogs, and a pleasure to train— very talented and can do any kind of work.

The Border Collie

The world's favorite sheepdog. All good Border Collies have a gathering style and varying amounts of "eye." At its best, a very exciting, biddable breed, but there are, unfortunately, some who don't work at all. Take care to get one from herding parents.

The Bouvier Des Flandres

The Bouvier was bred as a cowdog, and though most seem to show a gathering style, the rest are uninterested or are just stock-maulers. I feel they should be started on calves. Some are just too aggressive for a novice trainer. The better ones are good learners but can be stubborn, and a great deal depends on the determination of the trainer. I would not start this breed on ducks or sheep, though a few have done so with success. This breed can require stern corrections at times.

The Briard

Another breed whose shaggy "cuteness" sometimes attracts owners who don't want to develop the dog's very capable brain. The Briard is generally a gathering dog, and in the right hands is easily trained. Some are a bit aggressive at first, but learn quickly to modify that.

The Canaan Dog

Admittedly, one of my favorites. Israel's herder-guardian can be a first class herder—some have magnificent natural outruns. The Canaan can be quite independent and trainers of this breed should not hesitate to correct their dog if the situation calls for it. In the right hands, the Canaan uses his tremendous intelligence to do fantastic things with stock. In the wrong hands he uses that same intelligence to avoid doing what you want! Some Canaans are a bit aggressive with stock at first, but are fairly easy to tone down.

Caord Con's Black
Bison, C.D., in typical
Border Collie pose.
Breeder- owner, Janet
E. Larson.

C.C.A. Ch. Spatterdash Dreidle, T.D.,
Spatterdash Limor, C.C.A. C.D. (r). Ha'
Aretz Canaan Dogs. Bryna Comsky,
owner.

A Catahoula Leopard photographed by Carol Hamel Christiansen.

The Catahoula Leopard

The South's native herder is best started on calves or goats, though a few can be worked on ducks if they are not too aggressive. The "Cat" can be independent and needs to know that you are the leader. They are quite capable of learning anything and they don't really deserve their reputation of being just "wild-cow getters."

Collie (Show or Lassie Type)

There are many kinds of "Collies." The AKC Collie is primarily bred as a show dog today but a percentage still work, and those who do are gathering dogs. A few are just too big and awkward to outrun stock, but the right Collie can be a pleasure to train. Plan to take a fairly gentle approach with this breed as they are sometimes sensitive to criticism. They can be very smart and easy to train; a few are high strung.

The English Shepherds

A percentage of this breed gathers. I have seen really fantastic workers in this breed, and some that don't work at all. Buy a good one, from working parents. They are an all-purpose farm worker, not too classy but like the "old Chevy car," are very dependable and sturdy.

The German Shepherd

Germany's premier herder can still make a first rate sheepdog. Of the large numbers we have tested, probably 90 percent still retain herding instinct, and all of those seem to be gathering dogs. This shouldn't be surprising, since the ones worked in Germany must gather, drive, pen, and defend the flock! Some GSD are aggressive at first and require correction to modify this. They are very trainable and eager to please and can handle any kind of stock you have.

Atlion's Lisa Lox Mountie, U.D., SchH I owned by Jackie Atlion demonstrates the fetching or gathering instinct in German Shepherds.

Foxy, McNab owned by Donna Seigmund

Shetland Sheep-dog working ducks.

The McNab

This breed was *the* breed in California until the imported Border Collies nearly ousted them from trials. The McNab may not be as "classy" to watch work as their close relative, the Border Collie, but they are a good, tough range dog, and can go all day. Most are very willing dogs, easy to train but plenty tough when things get rough in bad terrain. All seem to be gathering dogs.

The Old English Sheepdog

Primarily a show dog, but a very small minority of them can work. Of those that do, most seem to be content to follow stock rather than gather, perhaps due to their size, weight and build. As a past drover's dog they were expected to be a herding "jack of all trades" and do all kinds of work (not just driving) so it is a shame that few of their owners want to work them. I have seen a few that were pretty stubborn, but others are quite biddable.

The Puli

This Hungarian herder can be quite talented, but not all of them will work. Some are totally disinterested, while others would work all day. Those who do work show a wide variety of styles—no one style seems typical. The breed is easy to train but care should be taken to get a bold one.

The Shetland Sheepdog

A lot of dog in a small package. The Sheltie, too, is mostly a show dog but many do still work, and some take several exposures to "turn on." The best ones seem to gather (though I've had a few in classes drive) and, of course, the worst do nothing at all. Shelties are easily trained and capable of being pretty tough if properly coached, but they seem best with ducks and smaller sheep. Some bark, and a few use "eye." They are very sensitive and should not be handled by anyone inclined to lose his temper.

Welsh Corgi (Cardigan and Pembroke)

I have grouped these two breeds together because of their close kinship and similarity of style. We all know the saying "dynamite comes in small packages," a phrase that applies well to these dogs. Some, of course, have lost the desire to work. But a large number do work, and, most surprisingly, many do gather. Given stock that is small enough (ducks or small sheep) the Corgis can gather and fetch stock with the best of them. They are fast learners and very biddable.

The Texas Heeler

Though not a true breed (they are the results of experiments in crossing the Australian Cattle Dog with the Border Collie), I am including them because they are popular and many of them are really dandy workers. Like the McNab they are not quite so classy as the Border Collie, but very gritty and most seem to gather and show a little "eye." They are "softer" than the pure Cattle Dog.

TEMPERAMENT IN THE HERDING BREEDS

We are very fortunate in that we who own herding breeds start with a big, big plus in our training. Herding breeds share many things in common, not the least of which is their temperament and with very few exceptions, a common ancestry.

Nearly all herding breeds were kept as close companions to man (unlike the guarding breeds which were often left alone with the sheep) and were bred over centuries to have a close rapport with their shepherd. Most shepherds direct their dogs in some manner, so herding breeds are quick to learn and eager to take direction once they know what you want. At the end of the day, these breeds went home with their shepherd or lay near him on the open land where the shepherd camped, and as a result, they are noted for their loyalty.

The more independent herding breeds either have been bred to work alone (i.e. the Catahoula Leopard often works for hours tracking wild stock out of sight of his master) or have not had the uninterrupted history of close association with man (i.e. the Canaan Dog was wild or semi-wild for many years before being revived and re-

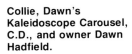
**Collie, Dawn's
Kaleidoscope Carousel,
C.D., and owner Dawn
Hadfield.**

**The Welsh Corgi can
work sheep with the
best of herders.**

domesticated). The Bouvier des Flandres and Australian Cattle Dog, and others bred to work cattle are a bit tougher and not as sensitive to tougher corrections.

You may have observed that most herding breeds do well in A.K.C. obedience. Their heritage of close association and training by humans is the primary reason for their success in these fields. Working dogs in the "olden days" that couldn't be trained didn't live to reproduce!

The herding breeds are nearly always eager to do what you ask, *once they understand what you are asking them to do*. It is up to us, then,

Whether independent or submissive in personality, all good sheep dogs are quick to learn and want to please.

to figure out how to communicate what we want. Before you complain that your dog will not mind, ask yourself how he could be confused. In my first cowdog class almost every student felt that their dog was stubborn and hard to train. By the end of the series of classes, all the students thought their dog was exceedingly smart! What happened? The dogs hadn't changed, but the owners had learned how to properly communicate with their dogs, who then were happy to obey!

Your dog is bred to please you, he wants to please you, and will please you. Herding dogs respond to praise, so let your dog know how pleased you are. You won't spoil him!

THE QUALITIES OF A HERDING DOG

Let's discuss some of the qualities we look for in a top herding dog of any breed. Make yourself familiar with these terms, as they are commonly used in America, Canada and Great Britain. Think of a whole dog as being a circle, and then picture that circle divided into equal parts, each contributing to the whole. That is what herding qualities are like—all must be present for the dog to be "whole" or really first-rate. If any part is missing, we would say that the dog has a fault as a worker, and describe it in terms relating to the whole. Now lets define some terms:

A power dog shows no fear of the stock.

Power

Power refers to your dog's self-confidence and self-assurance while he's working. Some dogs are very powerful, others are average and some lack power. A very powerful dog is a very assertive, confident dog that will walk right up to the stock and look them in the face, even touching noses with them—showing no fear or tendency to draw back. Many "power dogs" come on a little too strong at first because they just assume that the stock had BETTER move for them! A dog that lacks power, on the other hand, is unsure of itself and may draw back if challenged. The stock senses his insecurity and will often become offensive toward this dog. If challenged, some of these dogs will flee.

There is a crucial time in the training of some dogs when the trainer can make or break the dog's confidence, and some dogs who seem to lack power were made that way by wrong training. We will go into this more in the chapters on training.

Balance

A dog has balance if he's in the right place at the right time. Sometimes people use this term to refer to where the dog is in relation to the handler, but this is incorrect. Balance refers to the dog's position *on the stock*. If a dog is in balance, he can keep strays from happen--ing. A dog that is running too close, or splitting stock, is NOT in balance.

Concentration or "Eye"

"Eye" is a manner of approach in which the dog's intense concentration on the stock almost holds him back. A "strong eyed" dog drops his head on a level with his shoulder or below (some nearly drag their chin on the ground) and his approach is smooth and cautious. The "medium eyed" dog may drop his head and be quite intense, but moves more freely and less stylishly. The "loose eyed" dog does not drop his head, and is less intense than either of the previous dogs. The loose eyed dog is more inclined to glance around the field or watch his handler for directions, and nearly all barkers are loose eyed (that is to say, dogs that bark as they work).

Stewart Milne's Mac, showing eye.

It is not necessary for a dog to have ''eye'' to be a great worker, much to the unhappiness of those who insist that ''strong eyed'' dogs are the only way to go. Very few European breeds have ''eye'' and yet they are extremely capable workers. The reason probably is that their concentration is good, though not so intense as the strong eyed dog.

Desire To Work

The dog must want to work. Some dogs want to work so badly they would rather work than eat or sleep, while others enjoy working but are very easy to get to leave the stock. A dog that lacks the desire to work will never make an adequate herder. No dog trained mechanically (without instinct) ever makes a top performer and is totally incompetent when required to act quickly without command.

Temperament

Temperament is all important. We might add that a bold, outgoing dog usually makes a better herder than a shy or over-aggressive dog. A dog should be happy and comfortable with new situations, new livestock, and actually like the challenge herding brings. The dog should be well-bonded to its master, and be eager to please him or her. It is for this reason that most of the herding breeds have

This Australian Shepherd shows a good straight approach with intense concentration (eye). Down-Under's Tess of Bonnie - Blu, owned by Kathy and Tom Christian.

similar descriptions of temperament in their standards—an incorruptible character with a bold, confident approach to life.

Style

Style is a product of many qualities, usually power, balance, and degree of eye together with a good natural gather. Does the dog have an inborn desire to circle stock and bring them to its master? If so, how does he choose to do it? When you hear herding folk discuss "style" they are referring to a set of traits blending together.

Some dogs have everything going for them, but they don't really want to gather or even drive, they just sort of mess around or chase. If all other things are present, such dogs can be taught a style, and we will cover how to do this later, but keep in mind that such dogs are mechanical, and can never be trusted in emergency situations, when the slightest stress will cause them to revert to their natural behavior.

A Border Collie at work. (Photo by Edith Overly.)

3

Factors Affecting Starting Your Dog

Many things affect how and when you will start your dog. Though I often refer to "your pup" in this and following chapters, keep in mind that this applies to dogs of any age. In fact, I prefer to wait to start my own dogs until they are close to one year of age, or even later, depending on the dog's maturity. Some breeds do mature later than others. If you have a Beardie, Bouvier, or Old English, it pays to wait as long as you can. The optimum age for the late bloomers is fifteen to eighteen months, or even two years if you can hold off that long. Keep in mind that just because a dog *wants* to work, it doesn't follow that he *should* work right then—too much stress on undeveloped joints can cause great harm. (More on that further on.)

Let's look at the major factors that will tell you when and how to work your dog.

YOUR DOG'S BREEDING

By this I mean his age and bloodline. It goes without saying (but I'm saying it again), get the best dog from the best *working* line you can find. In some of the A.K.C. breeds this is a tough proposition, but it can nearly always be done. Look for a *using* line, at the very least; one that's been used for any kind of work, if not herding. However, my preference is always for a pup from proven herding parents because herding traits are extremely hereditary, and it is a lot less worrisome to not have to wonder whether the dog will work when it grows up. If the parents are herders, your chances of getting a herder increase to about 90 percent. Look for the kind of dogs you would like to own. Don't rush out and get the first dog you find. Buying a dog is like getting married—it pays to be darned sure! After all, you will have this dog, for better or worse, for many, many years. Investigate the breed, plug into the "hotline" of breeders that all breeds have. Find out who has working dogs. Ask for referrals.

In breeds where working is stressed, shop carefully. Buy a pup from parents that work the way you want your pup to work. Don't accept claims that one parent works but the other doesn't, but the breeder is SURE the pup will work! Don't expect one parent to be a miracle worker!

Allied with working ability is temperament. Buy the boldest, most confident pup. Shy dogs rarely make good herders. Then socialize your pup extensively; take it everywhere with you.

YOUR DOG'S AGE

A dog should be physically and mentally mature before you start herding. The bare bones minimum is six months, but if you can, wait

Never start a pup too young. Here a young pup gets a frightening challenge from an aggressive ewe.

even longer, since no pup is truly mature at six months. One year is ideal, but you can wait even longer. My own best herders have been dogs that weren't started until fifteen months of age or later. Some dogs simply don't start working until they're well over a year in age. This is called "late starting" or "slow coming into their work." One day you take your dog to the pasture and he shows no interest at all. The next day he may go completely bonkers over sheep and stay that way for the rest of his life. "Wait on Nature" is a favorite expression of some wise old sheepdog trainers. Let the dog tell you when he's ready, rather than try to force a response from him. Dogs started by coaxing and insistence rarely become the better herders. If you are impatient and have a choice, buy a pup from an early working line, rather than try to force a juvenile pup to do something he's plainly not ready for.

THE LIVESTOCK

The type of livestock to be worked can alter how you start your dog. Many young dogs are started on ducks, and hobbyists love ducks since they can even be kept in most cities. Take the trouble to get good stock for your dog to work—easy moving ducks or yearling whiteface ewes are usually good. Young dairy calves are another choice for the cowdogs. Try to get something that neither faces the dog and

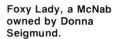

Foxy Lady, a McNab owned by Donna Seigmund.

attacks nor stampedes blindly in terror the moment a dog appears. Getting the right stock for the preliminary training is essential. Most stock can be sold at auction when you are ready for new animals.

Very tame, dog-broken stock is great for your pup's first few times out, but don't keep a dog on this sort of stock too long. It will give you a false sence of confidence, thinking that your dog is doing great things when, in fact, the animals are so tame that it doesn't matter what the dog does! This is really a problem for hobbyists working dogs in herding clubs that often keep a number of animals just for dog-work. These critters quickly learn the routine, and if used too long, your dog will not learn to correctly control range stock.

I am often asked what breeds of stock I recommend. Really, you may not get a choice, depending on your area, and a great deal depends upon how the stock was raised. I have seen sheep that were raised in an enclosure with a couple of dogs that they were able to bully, and they were impossible to work. My own preference (all things being as they should) right now is for Indian Runner or Runner Mallard cross ducks since they stay wild longer and cause the dog to run good and wide. Mallards are a close second choice. Avoid big, heavy ducks like Pekins and Muscoveys; they are too slow moving and will cause your dog to come in too close. In sheep I like any whiteface breed such as Dorset, Corriedale, Columbia, or Cheviot,

Very tame sheep are the choice for starting a young dog, but he should progress steadily to challenging sheep.

and cross-bred sheep with one of these breeds in them. If your dog is small (such as the Shelties and Corgis), stick with the smaller breeds—the Finn sheep, Cheviot, Southdown (their short legs do cause this breed to tire easier), or Karkul mixes.

THE WORKING AREA

A large area is best, even if you have to take some ducks, load them in a dog crate and haul them to your nearest park or playground. About one-half acre for ducks or an acre for sheep is good when starting, but plan to move into a bigger area later. Large areas make novice handlers nervous—they forget that their dog is bred to bring the stock back!

My preference is for a good sized area that is completely fenced around the perimeter with a fence the stock can't get through. This is more for your assurance than any real need. Most dogs, even untrained ones, will bring the stock back (albeit crudely) should they escape. If you can't find an area with a fenced perimeter (playground, Little League field, soccer field or your own backyard) for ducks or a fenced pasture for sheep, then you may have to use an open area, but plan to have family members or friends available in case you or your dog panics and the stock attempt to run.

PLEASE avoid working your dog in a tiny area, no matter what your excuse. Some trainers work in such small areas that their dogs NEVER learn to do any real work. Working in a small area is guaranteed to cause your dog to work much too close to his stock.

PHYSICAL CONDITION

Your dog should have sound hips, good eyes, and limbs free of deformity. A preliminary hip X-ray before you start working your dog can prevent a world of grief later. Those breeds with eye problems should be as clear as they can be for their age. It is cruel to get angry with a dog for not working well, only to discover that he can't see! Make sure your working prospect is sound before you start.

A more mature dog will be more coordinated, a big factor in herding. Your dog is an athlete and must be gradually worked up to his peak performance. It's not uncommon for beginning dogs to work for five minutes and then run out of steam. "Interval training" is the key word here. Work up gradually, over a period of months, and don't force your dog to keep going when he starts getting tired. Gradually condition his muscles so he will stay free of muscular pain and retain interest for a longer period.

Your own physical condition is also important. The obese often have trouble working a herding dog and should check with their doctor. You'll be doing plenty of running so good physical condition and proper running shoes are important.

TIME

The best sessions are short ones, five days per week. Sessions of fifteen minutes to one-half hour are typical. The bare minimum is one short session, three times per week. Do you have the time and dedication for this? If you are working fourteen hours a day, going to a night class and trying to spend time with your family, you may want to postpone starting your dog until things settle down. Don't start him and then put him up for months at a time as this only frustrates him.

Try to go into the session relaxed. When you first get home from work and are upset about something at the office is NOT the time to train your dog. If you're in a bad mood, hold off. Your dog should not become a scapegoat.

THE DOG'S RELATIONSHIP WITH IT'S TRAINER

No dog will give its best to a stranger, or even to a family member that it doesn't consider its master. Dogs must be strongly attached to their trainer. They must love and respect the trainer—qualities that will deepen and be enhanced as the training proceeds.

Some breeds will only work for their "love object" and the rest of the world can take a hike. Get to know your dog and help him to love and respect, not fear, you. Be kind, patient, but firm. Let him know that you are boss. You'll be expecting unusual obedience from your dog. There is no way you can MAKE a dog stop at one-half mile away.; he must *want* to do so in order to please you.

4
Is Your Dog Ready to Work?

Many novices ask, "How will I know my dog is ready to start?" There are several signs. A dog that is ready to start is eager when he sees the stock. When you turn him loose near the stock he makes attempts to circle them. These early attempts may be crude and may involve the dog splitting one off, running through the middle of the flock, etc., but his primary desire will be to *circle* or half-circle. A natural driving dog will follow stock, without circling. However, many natural gathering dogs do merely follow on their first exposures, until they gain confidence. Some dogs, if started too young, learn that they cannot outrun stock and so drop back and drive. Such dogs would have been gathering dogs, but early exposure "taught" them to do something else.

On the subject of starting dogs too young, there is one thing you should very carefully guard against doing. It has become faddish in the last few years to take young pups out to stock and let them chase and have a good time, all in the name of "interest building." I cannot make this point strongly enough—NEVER DO THIS! The damage it does to a pup is often irreparable. A young pup rarely has a mature herding style, but most puppies will chase and bite. In addition, their little baby legs *cannot* outrun the stock, and so they either chase or run in too close. Some of these dogs do work well enough to get to trials later, but they never turn in top performances in the higher level trials. Nearly all dogs started so young work too close and are very hard to get out wide, since they learned to run in too close at a very impressionable time. I have seen some really good pups turn out disasterously thanks to this ''puppy work.'' DON'T TAKE THE CHANCE WITH YOUR PUPPY.

A young dog eagerly circles the flock.

There is, of course, another problem of starting pups too young. If they are injured by the stock at an early age it is often the end of their working ability.

Here are some major signs that your dog is not yet ready to work:

- He is easily frightened of the stock. He acts fearful and bolts if they make a move toward him. Coupled with youth, this signals ''Not Ready.''

- Your dog is easily distracted. Some young dogs show great style for a minute or two, but are easily distracted by butterflys, or things on the ground. Even if your dog is a year old, put him up for a while longer and let him mature. Easy distraction is a sure sign of immaturity.

- He shows little or no interest in stock. Many good dogs show zero interest when they are young. Given time to grow up, they may really turn on. Never force your dog to work before he's ready. Some dogs sour if forced into herding.

WORK WITH YOUR DOG'S STYLE

Each breed works a little differently from every other breed, and you, as the trainer, must get to know what your breed, and your own dog, should be doing. Some breed clubs have Working Committees which have files of information. Other organizations, such as All-breed Stockdog Clubs, can be very helpful. Research all you can, read everything on your breed for clues, and don't accept rumor as fact.

The most important thing to remember is that you must work with the dog you have—you cannot force him to be something he wasn't bred to be. An example would be getting a Huntaway-style Beardie or Catahoula Leopard, then punishing it for using its voice when herding. Within these breeds, and many others, there is a whole set of standards as to how the dogs use their (as the British put it) *"noise and power."* It is cruel to get a dog bred to bark and then beat it for barking! Don't let anyone from another breed tell you that all herding dogs MUST behave a certain way, because it is not true. Those in the established breeds such as Border Collies or Aussies have often discouraged the novice starting out with a more "exotic" herder such as a Briard or Canaan because they don't work the same as a Border Collie.

Your dog is an individual, and should be allowed a certain amount of expression of his own unique style. If your dog works in a slow canter, instead of a fast gallop, *but it works for him*, let him do so! If your Aussie barks instead of bites when sheep challenge, but they respect him just as much, *and it works for him*, then let him do it this way. The key is, does it work? One of my favorite dogs is a young Beardie that I have been showing in trials. He is a "Huntaway" (barker) and we've been competing in predominantly Border Collie

This close working Aussie shows that "good style" is relative—close working is only a fault when it disturbs the sheep. Here the sheep are held in perfect control.

trials. This dog barks incessantly, yet he works good and wide and can move stock from a far greater distance than a strong-eyed dog. Most of the Border Collie trials judges were candid with me that they didn't like the barking (not being used to it) but that they could not deny this dog his proper award because he did his job and had a *positive effect on the stock*. That is the name of the game.

Some things are universally bad. Mauling the stock, sharp flanking, quitting, etc., are NOT part of a dog's personal style but are reflections of temperament and should always be discouraged. Ask yourself, "Is what my dog is doing having a positive effect on the stock? Are they moving calmly and quietly, showing no fear, and staying well grouped?" If the answer is "Yes," then even if your dog does something that you don't find appealing (such as glancing around the field, or never completely putting his rear all the way down when you stop him), allow him a little free expression. Every dog has personal quirks. Another example is that same huntaway Beardie has a habit of looking about the field at times. Since Huntaways are used in Britain to gather hiding stock, this is not surprising. Most of the time I don't care for this habit, but once some stock got out and no other dog saw them except this dog, and he brought them back from some very rough territory. Except for the fact that he was always looking and sniffing the air, he would have missed their escape. Learn

Singling one animal off from the herd and chasing it must be stopped right at the beginning. This stems from the dog's primitive hunting behavior.

to appreciate your dog's best qualities and his ecentricities. He is unique and should not be forced into a mold.

As you grow as a trainer, you will begin to know your dog better than you ever believed possible. Some trainers see nothing but bad in their dogs, while others can see nothing but good. Try to strike a balance and appreciate your dog's best qualities while being objective about the areas where he needs work.

The author's Beardie, Tweed, brings the ducks up.

SOME RULES TO FOLLOW

1. Never let your dog work on his own.

Why should your dog obey you if he knows he can have more fun without you? Dogs that work on their own, unsupervised, pick up habits which are impossible to break. Don't risk it. Establish the fact that you are a team.

2. Remember to tap the cane ON THE GROUND continuously.

Your dog can't see the cane if you hold it in the air. The point of using the cane is to keep the dog running wide, off the stock. USE it.

3. Protect the livestock at all costs.

Never let your dog harm an animal. We will allow many little quirks but never, ever allow your dog to do harm while he works. A dog must be a help, not a hinderance.

4. Once you have stopped the dog, never allow him to get up until you release him.

In the beginning training, YOU make the decisions about when and where your dog will get up. Later on, you will trust your dog's judgement at times, but dogs that have been allowed to pop up whenever they feel like it are impossible to stop.

5. Never do "dry work" without stock.

This is boring and makes your dog mechanical. Don't do it.

6. Do not give too many or meaningless commands.

Many novices get nervous and use too many words that their dog doesn't understand and therefore learns to ignore. While working

The handler reaches down to catch a ewe, dog moves up aggressively. Catching sheep will bring out a dog's predatory behavior, which must be discouraged.

your dog, say only things that will have an effect on his training. I have heard many novices repeat a whole stream of things to their dog; "Go bye, good boy, that's the stuff, go left, what a good dog, oh, are you smart," etc. etc. Stick to the basic commands and praise words your dog will come to recognize. You can repeat certain commands, but don't clutter your speech too much. Keep it simple.

7. Do give verbal praise.

I have heard a few trainers say they never praise their dogs. However, their dogs don't learn as quickly as dogs trained with praise. Working is NOT its own reward. Like a child, your dog has to learn right from wrong. Help him by praising him when he is doing the right thing. Men seem to have more trouble with praise and enthusiasm while training, but they can learn to overcome this problem.

8. NEVER use hand signals!

Many people unconsciously gesture as they work their dogs, and others do so because they think they should. Hand signals cause the dog to look at you, but we want his eyes on the stock at all times, while he listens for your spoken or whistled commands. Dogs trained with hand signals get into real trouble when worked at a distance, since their vision is very poor (but their hearing is very good). You can wave and point all you want in a snowstorm, heavy rain or fog, but a dog cannot see you from very far away. BUT HE CAN HEAR, especially a whistle, at distances. There have never been _any_ top trial dogs trained on hand signals! Learn from their example.

9. Never call your dog off in the middle of a working session.

Don't call your dog off in the middle of working just to prove you can. And don't use the call off as a way to give yourself time to think, or to stop a situation that's going downhill.

An exception to this occurs later in the dog's training when you will call him off to send him on an outrun. By then your dog will learn what to expect. Calling him off too much during his early training can cause him to be hesitant about going out (he expects to be called back) or to quit intermittently (he has learned from you that stick-to-it-iveness has no value.

A dog running too close on his outrun will send sheep on the run—a fault.

5
Some Herding Terms

We will be using these terms throughout this book, so it is important that you fully understand their meaning.

FLANKING OR FLANKING COMMANDS — The commands given to direct the dog around the stock, either to the left, right, or full circle. The dog is flanking the stock when he is moving to either side around them. He is not flanking when he is coming straight on to them. *Wide flanking* refers to a dog working on these commands wide off the stock. *Sharp flanking* is the act of the dog coming in too close (usually at high speed), and sometimes touching the stock as he moves. Sharp flanking is a common problem and a fault.

Flanking commands from handler to dog help guide the sheep to the correct destination.

OUTRUN — The outrun is a semicircular run the dog makes to get to the far side by going out behind the stock. He should go out and around far enough to the other side so as not to disturb the stock. There are many different kinds of outruns. The *acceptable* outruns are:

The semi-circle—just as it says, a wide semi-circle.

The Pear-shaped—smaller, close to the handler and wider as the dog nears the stock, like the shape of a pear.

Faulted outruns include: The box shaped, where the dog runs the fence lines without paying attention to where his sheep are; the total circle, where the dog runs the whole field in a circle and ends up in back of the handler; and cross over or too straight outrun, where the dog changes the side he's running on or runs straight at the sheep.

The goal of the outrun is to get the dog behind (to the other side of) the sheep speedily and out wide enough from them that (ideally) they don't even spot him until he starts his approach. With this goal in mind, you can see that the dog expends too much energy when he follows the fence line. In the full circle the dog doesn't stop behind the sheep, but instead runs all the way back—very counter-productive! In the outrun where the dog crosses over, he runs a big risk of the sheep seeing him coming from the wrong side, and stampeding them the wrong way—away from the handler. Likewise the too straight

Acceptable Outruns:

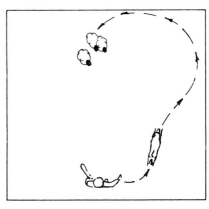

Semi-circle.   Pear shaped

outrun, where the dog goes charging up the middle, usually stampeding the sheep and often splitting them, has the effect of a cue ball breaking a bunch of closely packed pool balls.

The most common outrun problems the novice has are with his dog crossing over or running too straight. We'll talk about why when we get into the training of the outrun, but suffice to say that a good, clean semi-circle or pear-shaped outrun is your goal.

Faulty Outruns:

Box shaped

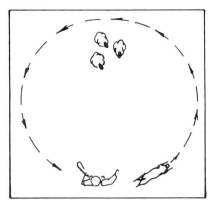

Total circle

Cross-over

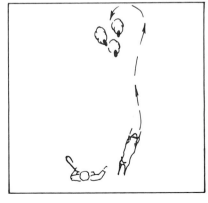

Too straight

The Lift — The lift is the dog's introduction to the stock—when they first become aware of a dog approaching them. It is a fleeting few seconds, but it is important since the sheep take their cue from how the dog acts at this time and they react accordingly. A steady, cautious lift from the dog (moving in slowly but confidently, without charging in or acting wild or hesitant) is important to convince the sheep to respond as they should.

The Fetch — This commences after the lift and is when the sheep realize the dog is coming on to them and they begin to move away from the dog. Depending on what moves the dog makes, the sheep should come toward the handler. A straight line is most desirable. Why? Take a look at the diagrams. Which sheep are using up the most energy (burning expensive feed)? If you guessed the ones going in the straightest line to the handler you are correct! They use less energy and waste less time, don't they? This is important since no one wants to feed stock more than you really need to, and no one likes to take all day just moving the stock from point ''a'' to boint ''b,'' so we strive to teach our dogs a *straight* fetch.

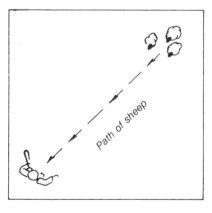

A straight fetch

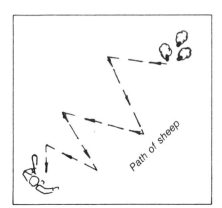

An incorrect fetch

Approach — This is how the dog moves toward the stock. Is he steady and calm, but confident? Is he bouncey and uncertain? Is he blustery and over-excited? All these things are described in the word "approach." A steady, calm, but confident approach is the best. Such a dog conveys competence to his stock, without making them fearful or suspicious.

(*Top*) **The lift is the dog's introduction to the stock.**

(*Bottom*) **Belgian Sheepdog, owned by Chuck Eklot, shows the breed's natural gathering style.**

Wide Running and Close Running — These refer to the distance the dog is from the stock as he works.

A "wide running" dog moves around his stock, keeping a good distance away from them. He almost seems to get a charge out of dazzling us with his speed as he circles.

A "close running" dog moves very close to the stock, sometimes close enough to almost touch them. Most novices have a problem of their dogs running too close rather than too wide because most herding breeds are naturally close running dogs that must be trained to run wide. There are exceptions, usually found in Border Collies, Kelpies, and Beardies.

Wearing — The "pendulum" motion a dog makes, moving from side to side, to push stock forward and keep them grouped.

Re-direction — A dog taking a new command or, a dog taking a command against his natural instinct, obeying because you ask him to.

Bearded Collie, Scot, moves dairy heifers to pasture. Wearing is most beneficial on large herds or flocks.

6

Starting Your Dog

EQUIPMENT NEEDED

So you have decided to start the training. First let's look at the supplies you need. The first thing is an 8 to 10-foot-long bamboo pole (preferably green bamboo). If bamboo is not available in your area (either growing wild or in nurseries) then a thin piece of plastic PVC pipe (available at home supplies and hardware stores) is a good second choice. Look at the thicknesses and get one that will be easy for you to handle. PVC is heavier than bamboo. On no account use the common, short shepherd's cane or crook for the training phase, though they are lovely trial canes, just for show. They are too heavy and should you tap this on the ground, and your dog runs into it, it can really hurt him. So put the show canes away for training time.

You will need a choke chain collar (the kind used in obedience) and a good strong leather lead. It is a good idea to get a 20-foot piece of clothesline for the dog to drag a bit in his early training. Later you may want to get a whistle. DON'T get the common police type whistle—it will destroy your eardrums, not to mention your dog's! You can buy plastic whistles that are made in Britain from suppliers, or you can buy a boson's pipe at boating and marine supplies (they work extremely well) or get a common Hartz Mountain plastic whistle at the grocery store. Don't buy the "silent" type whistles: they collect lint in your pocket. Occasionally the bottom of this whistle will unscrew without you realizing it, making the sound impossible for the dog to hear. Since you do not know he can't hear it, you could correct the dog unjustly. Start off with a whistle you *both* can hear well without blasting your ears.

THE STEPS TO STARTING A DOG

The old adage "every dog is different" applies well to sheep dog training. Although the format I am about to describe is my favorite, it should be borne in mind that sometimes, with some dogs, you have to switch things around. Not every dog is the exact blend we want at first. Some dogs are very hard and aggressive, others are very soft.

My *ideal* is to try to train in the order listed. The most common reason I vary it is if the dog is very soft and I feel that teaching the stop very early on might kill the dog's interest. I will then teach the flanking commands before the stop, or try to get the dog to pause at the word "there." The soft dogs need lots of confidence-building experiences. They are like a person who has no faith in his abilities. You need to build his interest and feelings of competence so high that

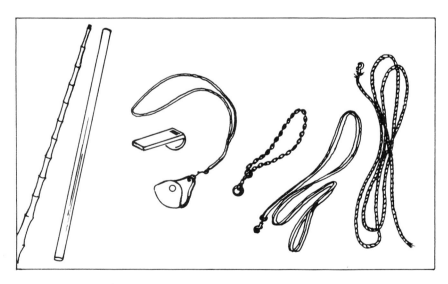

Basic herding equipment (l to r): a tapered bamboo pool, plastic pipe, two types of whistles, chain choke collar, 6 ft. leash, and 20 ft. clothesline lead with snap.

putting harder commands on him will no longer fase him. But don't let your dog fool you, either. You should know if your dog is genuinely soft--if he is hypersensitive to criticism. If he normally is not soft, but acts that way on stock, try to find out why before you label him soft.

Some dogs start out aggressively at first, but learn to settle down; some dogs start out soft and learn to be much "harder." Most dogs, however, will fall somewhere in the middle range, able to take a certain amount of constructive criticism so long as they receive praise for correct behavior.

If you are working with a dog of very hard temperament, one that comes on strong and is hard to handle, my advice would be to start applying the stop earlier than the two weeks I will be suggesting. It may help you get a handle on him. The very aggressive dog doesn't mind correction, and is usually so interested in working that you could set off firecrackers in the field while he was working and he would hardly notice.

One reason I list the training in the order that follows is that, in my own experience, this order best provides for true all-breed training. It has worked the best in classes where we had a wide variety of herding breeds. If at any time your dog seems confused and you are not making progress, go back to the last lessons to review and reinforce what he CAN do, then try to figure out how he became confused.

Always remember—you are the more intelligent one in this training relationship. If your dog is not learning what you want him to, ask yourself "What have _I_ done or not done that has confused him?" Too many people blame their dog, but all dogs (especially the herding breeds) want to please the one they love. You must figure out what message your dog has been getting, and then correct it by presenting the message in a way that is easier for him to understand. Be quick to follow this approach, and stop blaming your dog when things go wrong.

TEACHING THE DOG TO STOP AND COME (DRY WORK)

The first lessons are taught away from stock, which is the reason it is called "dry work." Aside from the stop, come, and possibly, later, the get back, never do any other dry work. You often hear of Aussie trainers going to rather elaborate methods of putting the dog on a line and then making it walk circles around the handler, back and forth, while the handler repeats the commands over and over. This is not only boring, it is damaging to your dog, and will make him mechanical. You can always tell dogs that have been trained without instinctive motivation (you see, this type of dry work has nothing as a "pay off" for the dog—no stock to move). Dogs trained a lot with dry work are always far more mechanical in their responses than those that have been trained with their instinct. Some of these dogs will turn around and look at their handler while the stock charges off, since the dog wasn't watching it.

It is very important for you to remember to always have a "payoff" for your dog. During the teaching of the stop and come, that payoff is praise (and sometimes for the stop, a ball or frisbee). YOU MUST PRAISE THE DOG WHILE HE IS DOING THE RIGHT THING, NOT AFTERWARDS. Your dog can't recall that five minutes ago he stopped and that is why you are praising him now. He will think he is getting praise for the most current thing he did (which may not be at all what you want). So praise, *as the dog is lying down*, praise *as the dog comes to you*, etc. Associate the praise with his performance.

As your dog is learning these commands, do not combine the "Stop" and "Come." When you do this it confuses your dog, so that he thinks they are always combined. The end result of this is that your dog comes to you to lie down! So do Downs for awhile, then later in the day do "Comes," or vice versa.

TRAINING THE "COME"

Even the youngest pup of twelve weeks or so can begin the "come" training. At this age it is always a fun thing, with lots of praise and *no* correction. Attach a long clothesline to the puppy's collar. I am assuming your puppy is now used to wearing his collar and going along on a lead. If not, do these things first, until your puppy is comfortable with them. You can't teach him to come if he's terrified of being on a line. So now you have the pup on this line, and just drop back any way you choose to go, saying pup's name, "COME" in a _light, happy voice_. The pup will probably come, just to see why you made those sounds; if he doesn't, just reel him gently in, and when he reaches you, reach (or bend) down and praise, stroking his head and repeating "Good dog, COME, COME." Let him hear the command, and associate it with the pleasure of having his head stroked.

This should be done for several weeks, preferably a few times per day. All you are after is to help your pup associate the word "Come" with pleasant things. Need I add that you NEVER, EVER call a dog to you to punish it? Many ranchers make this mistake and then are perplexed as to why their dog runs away when they call it. Give your dog praise for coming and he will learn to come; punish your dog for anything, after calling him, and you teach him not to come at all. We will get into the correction for NOT coming soon, but just remember that you _never_ call your dog to punish it. You _always go to it_ to correct.

To teach a very young pup to come, kneel down and clap your hands or call to him.

Walk around in new areas with your pup on this clothesline and practice calling him. He will be distracted by new sights and will be more inclined to ignore you. Continue reeling him in, and praising him for coming to the command. He may not be actually coming to the command, but after weeks of practice he will.

When you are 100% sure he understands, and your pup is at least four months old, you may begin to correct him if he doesn't come. Do not apply the correction unless you have been practicing for at least two weeks without it (especially for very young pups, and untrained older dogs). Applying correction too soon is sure to frighten your dog, especially if he doesn't understand why he's being corrected.

Now that your dog understands the Come command, you can walk him about with the full length of the clothesline extended, so that he can drift away 20 feet or so. Now call the dog with the usual command Pup's Name, "COME." If he does come, praise lavishly. If he doesn't come, keep the line in your hand and *go to him quickly*, taking hold of the tip of his ear with your free hand and giving it a pinch. SAY NOTHING AS YOU CORRECT. As soon as you have

Teaching the "Come." Reel in, and praise the dog when he gets to you.

completed the correction (don't monkey around, do the whole thing in seconds) then immediately step back _a couple of feet_ and repeat the command. Chances are, at this distance your dog will come, and when he does, praise very lavishly including the word "Come" in your praise. If he doesn't, just reel him up to you and praise anyway. Don't pinch the ear again.

What you are trying to get across is that when the pup comes on command very happy things happen to him, but when he doesn't come, bad things happen. You give him the chance to do it right immediately after the correction so that he gets the contrast. Many of my obedience friends marvel at the fast, exuberant recalls of my dogs and those of my students. The reason is that our dogs are very clear on how happy the "COME" really is, and how unpleasant not coming is! It is extremely important that your dog get the contrast, and have the chance to do it right after each and every correction.

In practicing this, do not drop the line until your dog is coming well every time. When you think he has the message, drop the line and let him drag it. At the moment when he least expects it, call him. If he comes, praise him; if he doesn't, go to him (even if you have to step on the line to keep him from running around), do the correction, then immediately step back and call him _while holding_ the line. This ensures that the second time he will obey, and you won't have to correct again and again.

The ear pinch is a tough correction but a little goes a long way. You don't want to hurt the dog, just get his attention. Soft dogs will sometimes give a yelp of shock when first you do it, so you must counter with loads of happy praise when the dog obeys. On the other hand, some very hard dogs act like nothing at all bothers them. I've had a few very tough, thick-skinned dogs in classes (especially a few Bouviers and Catahoulas) that totally ignored the ear pinch, or whose owners couldn't get a hold of a cropped ear buried in lots of hair. For those dogs, we used either a large link choke chain, or prong collar. In the place of the ear pinch, a jerk on the collar is administered to these dogs when they don't obey. Then the owner steps back as usual and calls the dog, praising it when it does come. Lest anyone think this is cruel, let me tell you that a couple of these dogs would knock down and drag their owners (it goes without saying we used a horse longe line rather than a thin little clothesline on these big guys) all over through the dirt, and one would attack his owner whenever he tried to get the dog to do *anything*. These dogs might take off running, trying to attack other dogs in class or running into traffic. Sometimes, in the case of a very, very tough dog, tougher measures are needed. It's far kinder to teach the dog to come than to have a huge dog totally out of control and a menace to himself and others. If you have problems, consult a professional trainer.

Gradually you will progress to no lead or line at all, although at first this should be done in an enclosed area so the dog can't run off if you must go to him to correct. Never forget the praise for doing it right!

If you have children or other family members eager to help, be *sure* they understand that they must not call the dog unless they are able to follow through if the dog disobeys. Children are probably the best socializers of puppies I've ever known, but the younger ones can accidently un-train a dog from coming by calling him and, if he doesn't come, just shrugging it off and forgetting it. Better to have the young children *not* call the dog rather than have this happen. Or, you can do as we have in this house—kids can say anything *but* Dog's Name, "COME"—they call the dog with "here." That way, when an adult says "COME," the dog knows he means it.

TRAINING THE "DOWN"

The next command is to have the dog lie down. There is much controversy over whether a dog should lie down, sit or stand to stop while he's working. Personally, I greatly prefer a dog that will stop and stand on his feet, but I rarely teach this to a young dog right off the bat, mainly because young, keen dogs just don't stop and stand. It's easier to teach the dog to lie down at first, and over a period of months let him "fudge" and only stand or sit. What I often do is teach the dog to "down" and then, when he is being allowed to stop and stand I use the word "there."

You can use any sort of command to stop your dog—"down," "stop," "drop," "wait," etc.; all work well. Use whatever comes naturally to you, and be sure always to use this same command each time.

1. Place the leash under your foot and one hand on the dog's shoulder.

2. Press down on the dog's shoulder while pulling up on the lead.

3. When the dog is completely down, keep foot on lead and praise lavishly. Do not release dog until you say "get-up."

To start this command, get a proper sized chain collar (choke chain) and be sure it is big enough with large enough links so your dog can feel it. Often, my students attend their first class with collars on their dogs that wouldn't stop a Toy Poodle, much less a good-sized, over-keen young dog. Some of the newer "fur saver" choker chains, alas, just don't do the job. If your dog is small and hypersensitive (many Shelties fall into this category) then one of these collars may do the job, but for most breeds, getting a fairly hefty collar is necessary.

If your dog is already *highly* obedience trained, you will want to use another type of collar, so your dog won't think he's doing a new obedience lesson. Sometimes these dogs are maniacs on stock, forgetting their obedience lessons totally, but more often they are slightly inhibited at first, so there is no need to confuse them with collars. Use a nylon slip-type collar or even a flat leather collar for herding, and leave the chain collars for obedience. If you haven't used a chain collar for obedience, then by all means use one for herding.

The first lessons should be done in a calm, distraction-free place with the dog on a leather-type lead and wearing his collar so that the "active" ring (the one that does the snapping and releasing) is facing your side. For about a week, you will place the lead under the middle of your foot and, while pulling up on the lead, push down on the dog's shoulder. (*See photos.*) When he is down, keep him down by keeping your foot tightly on the lead. Praise the dog and repeat "DOWN" or whatever command you are using, again and again, perhaps stroking his head as you do. *Do not let him up* until *you* release him. The almost universal command for this is "Get up," but anything will do. Then let the dog up and *praise him for getting up.* You are actually teaching him to get down *and* get up. *Never* let the dog get up without permission.

When the dog is down, keep him down for thirty to sixty seconds, praising him all the while. This makes him more familiar with the position. Timing is important. Don't struggle with him to get him down; try to get him down within one or two seconds of saying the command. You want an *instant* response. The dog is supposed to drop like a brick the second you say the command.

For those of you with big, unruly dogs, pressing down on their shoulders while pulling the lead as described may only serve to get the dog bucking like a horse. My advice is to start right away with either a snap correction, or try grabbing the dog's front legs and pulling them out, while someone else pulleys the lead from the other side of the dog. (*See photos.*)

Now that your dog is familiar with the command, and has a hazy idea of what it's about, you will start to show him that you mean business about this new word: that "down" means "down, right *now*." This is probably the *only* command in herding that uses a bit of force in the training, because it is so very vital. It is the command all others are predicated upon, and the way you have to control the speed of your dog and the speed of the stock. Pay special attention to the timing as described, since it makes the difference between a snappy, instant stop and one that may or may not work (the dog stops when he feels like it.)

Stand with both hands on the leather lead with your dog wearing his chain collar attached to the lead. Give the command "Down" and count (fast) to one. If your dog isn't down all the way by then, give a sharp jerk (downward, not toward you) with the lead. This will cause your dog to be down, and he may be slightly confused. IMMEDIATELY praise lavishly for his being down! Do not release him until you say "get up." You want to counter any hurt feelings he may have over the correction by immediately letting him know how happy you are with his fast down. A note of caution—when saying "Down," keep your voice light, happy and soft. Your dog doesn't need to be yelled at, and yelling or sounding stern may make him think of the down as a correction. It is tempting to shout when you are preparing for correction but *don't. Always* keep your voice conversational, except when you use your voice for correction. Also, *never, ever* repeat the "down" as you correct. This is guaranteed to make him think of the down as a correction while you want him only to associate it with praise. So *say nothing* when you correct, but praise lavishly when the dog obeys.

Timing is critical in this lesson. Do not fumble around with the lead while your dog frolics about, ignoring your command. *Do* give the dog time to respond: don't say "Down" and then lower the boom on him before he can start to lie down. You want him down fast and without any wasted time, but remember that a big, heavy dog may need an extra second or two to get his larger bulk down. A Bouvier can hit the dirt pretty fast, but he won't be as fast as a Sheltie.

As your dog responds to this snap-correction with his collar, let the lead out so you can walk around the yard. Some dogs take this lesson to heart and refuse to get up. If your dog does this, pull him up and then praise him equally lavishly for getting up. Some dogs will try to come toward you to lie down. This is often the fault of the trainer, who may unconsciously be pulling the dog toward himself as he jerks down. If you haven't been doing this, but your dog tries to come to you, tie him to a fence or have someone else hold him, use the command, and *then go to the dog* to correct him. Praise him for being down, release him, then walk off. If you are very coordinated, another way is to let the dog drag a lead in a fenced yard, and give the command. When the dog disobeys, *go to him* (and do it fast, before he has the chance to start moving toward you). Correct him, then praise him for being down, let him lie there for a minute in the down position, then release him with "Get up." Praise him for getting up.

The down can in practical use to prevent the Border Collies from moving stock too fast. (Photo by D. Reinke)

Once your dog is *thoroughly* familiar with the "down" command, you will progress to the next stage. Let the dog drag a light cord around the yard, and give the command to down when he least expects it. At this phase you can always get a hold on him if you need to correct him, either by stepping on the line or by catching it with your hands. After a period of weeks, you will let the dog loose in the yard (still wearing his chain collar), and practice this exercise with no lead or line.

When the dog is doing well off the line in the yard, start adding distractions, and let him drag his leather lead. My dogs love to play ball, frisbee and tug of war with an old sock. These are great distractions to practice with. Throw the ball, and just before the dog gets to it, tell him to down. After you have gone to him and praised him for downing, let him get the ball as part of his reward. Or tease the dog with his old sock, get him really excited (but don't let him have it) and then tell him to down. Once he's down, release him and as he gets up, let him grab the sock and play a bit. Some of my students incorporate the down into just playing with the dog. While taking the dog for runs at the park they would command the dog to down, right in full stride. After lavish praise for downing, the dog is released and off and running again! These distractions are good, because they teach the dog that downing is *fun*, not a punishment. Also, since livestock isn't involved, you can come in hard on the corrections if you need to, without souring the dog on livestock. Some dogs would just turn off if you started this type of correction when they were working stock since at the beginning their instinct may hang by a thread. But by correcting them with an old favorite—sock, ball playing at the park, etc.,—you don't run as great a risk, and there is no way they will associate the correction with stock.

If you intend to use a hiss or a whistle to stop your dog, you may want to introduce this now. Whistle (one short blast) or hiss just *before* you give the "down" command. Like Pavlov's dog, soon your dog will hear this sound and anticipate your down command; so he will down. I use both a hiss and the word "down" in close to my dogs while they work, and whistles to work them farther away. But I start all mine out with a hiss and a vocal command.

When your dog is doing well, keep practicing all the time. The more he does it (and gets praise for it), the better he will like it and respond.

Denise Leonard and Kirk at Cummington, Mass., Sheepdog Trial.

7

Introducing the Dog to Stock

This lesson is the hardest for trainers, and the easiest for the dogs! This is the part that most novice handlers feel is most difficult; it makes them feel uncoordinated and dumb. In fact, a few never do learn it and their dogs never get trained. For the first times out, prearrange everything for success. Have your bamboo pole (or PVC) handy, have your dog on a flat leather collar with a long cord attached to it (he will drag this so you can catch him easily) and put your stock into a good sized, open area, free of bushes, trees, etc., and also free of distractions. The area should be fenced along its perimeter, but it must be large enough for you and your dog to hold your stock in the open, rather than along the fence.

For the handler, this lesson consists of walking around in a circle (walking *forward*, not side to side like a crab), while tapping the cane from side to side (*See photos.*) If you think this will be hard for you to recall when the action gets thick, practice it without the dog or stock. (You may want to do this where your neighbors can't see you, it looks pretty funny!)

I often have students practice this without a dog, to build their confidence. The point of this cane work is:

1. To protect the stock from being "dive bombed" by your dog;

2. To teach the dog to run around the stock in a circle (thus *you* walk around the stock, tapping the cane ahead of you, to keep the dog circling and away from being too close to the stock).

3. To let the dog bring the stock toward you (while you tap the cane from side to side to keep the dog from going the wrong way) as you walk backward.

Rogues Hollow Great Scott begins training on ducks. (Note bamboo pole used to block dog from coming in too closely.)

Walk forward around stock as you tap the cane to get the dog circling wide.

Improper use of the cane — note how dog is flanking in too sharply because cane is held out straight in the air (out of dog's eyeview). Tapping the cane on the ground is more effective.

Let us take a close look at what your dog is trying to do.

Your goal the first several times out is to teach your dog to "run a pattern." That is, get it set in his mind that he is to circle and semi-circle stock and keep them moving toward you. Your goal is not only to teach him that, but also to do it *properly*; nice and wide from his stock.

At this time your dog is building interest in this work, and it would be a grave mistake to try to start into obedience training now. Besides, no novice trainer can do everything at once, so for the dog's first attempts say *nothing* but "Good dog!". Don't call him, don't try to make him down; nothing but "Good dog!." If the dog tries to flash in and nip at the stock, speak sharply to him using a particular sound; I like "Ah!" said very sharply. As you say this, slap the cane *hard* on the ground in front of the dog. If he has already grabbed one of the animals, slap the cane on his toes. When he backs off, praise him.

Many dogs will run wild in their first attempts, while others act disinterested. For those that run wild, you will use the cane very vigorously; *tap* the cane *hard* on the ground to protect your stock. Let the dog see that it would be very unpleasant to run into that cane. Don't stop slapping the cane long enough for your dog to dash in. If he then chooses to come in too close and runs into your cane, he will learn the hard way how unpleasant it is. I prefer to use green bamboo as it bends easily and will give the dog a little thump but not hurt him if he does run into it. Always remember that your dog has a *choice* here. It is *his* choice to run in too close, and he will learn on his own (with a little help from you) what the consequences are.

If your dog is disinterested, carry your cane but don't slap it on the ground. Move the stock around yourself, act excited about them and praise your dog for any positive move he makes. Some dogs take several exposures, so if your dog doesn't "turn on" the first time, bring him out the next day, and the next, and so on. *Don't* lose your patience with him, and *don't* try to force him to herd by dragging him around by the collar or yelling for him to come back if he stops to sniff the ground.

The natural instinct of one of the fetching or gathering breeds is to keep the stock between you and him at all times. That is why he runs around to the other side of the stock. You can utilize this throughout your training by walking *around* the stock, and noticing how your dog runs around to the other side to balance you. If you walk around the stock, and also away from them (toward your dog a bit) you will force him out wider, especially so if you are slapping your cane. The sequence of slapping the cane must be constant. The dog should try to avoid the slapping cane. *Don't* stand there, clutching the cane without moving it! Keep the tip of the cane always tapping the ground.

So your dog is running around the stock, you are walking forward around the stock (see diagrams for teaching directions), and you should remember to switch sides (walk around the other way) every two turns or so, otherwise you and your dog may get dizzy. Most dogs want to move stock, and not just run around them in a big circle, so when you see that your dog is staying back off them, start to walk backward, tapping the cane from your left to your right side, to hold the dog on the far side of the stock from you, and to prevent him from running a full circle *in front* of you (crossing between you and the stock). The latter, called ''ringing'' is a serious fault. If your dog does this, slap the cane very hard to make him think twice about coming around in front of you. If he gets around and makes a full circle behind you at this stage it's okay, but never let him cross in front of you!

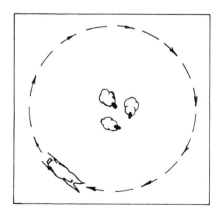

"Go Bye" Handler walks clockwise.

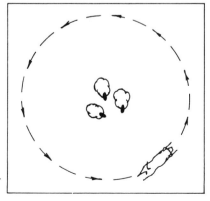

"Away to Me" Handler walks counter-clockwise.

Good use of a long PVC pole in early training by Dawn Hadfield with her Collie, Dawn's Kaleidoscope Carousel, C.D.

As you give ground (walking backward) the stock will be inclined to move toward you. Most livestock is equally afraid of humans as they are of a dog, so you must not stand there and expect your poor dog to put some very nervous stock in your lap. It's very easy to get caught up with the idea of "Wow! My dog is *working*!" and forget where you are. I have had some students tell me that walking backward, tapping the cane, saying "Good dog" and not falling over something was almost more than they could handle. A month later these same students laugh at how easy it all becomes; sort of second nature.

The first few times will undoubtedly be less than you had hoped for, but be patient and persistent. If your dog is keen to "run" on the stock, let him stay at this stage for about fourteen times out. By the end of this period you should have it more together with your cane and all, and your dog will be keen enough to start taking and learning commands. If your dog's interest is still tentative, however, wait longer to start the commands and keep building him up, telling him how much you love it when he does good things with the stock.

If your dog is very tentative about his interest, go to the flanking commands *first*, before the stop command. Teaching the dog the stop (which requires a little correction) can sour a dog that hasn't fully committed himself to working. But if your dog is the more common, enthusiastic sort, proceed to the next lessons.

TEACHING THE STOP ON THE STOCK

For some trainers, this is the hardest of all the lessons. Once you get this one, everything else is easy, because this is the only inductive command used in herding. This means that all the other commands are taught by utilizing the dog's natural instinct and the "stop" command is the only one that *doesn't* come naturally to your dog. This command is our safety valve and the only way we can control the dog's speed (which translates into the speed of the stock).

At this point you have a dog that eagerly runs around stock and also toward them, bringing them toward you as you walk backward. When you are sure nothing would kill his interest, start to apply the stop (down) command.

To start with, make sure you are in a big enough area so he can get around the stock, but small enough so you don't have to run over 25 acres to catch him. Put on the chain collar with the long cord attached. *Before you go in to work the stock, practice the down command for about 15 minutes.* If you're working with a friend, don't let him watch other dogs work. Just walk around, making sure that the dog is stopping perfectly. If he isn't, keep practicing. *Don't* take the dog in until he stops perfectly.

The first time I apply this command I get a few of the "bugs" out of the dog first. I let him circle and run around the stock for several minutes, doing our usual routines until he has the edge off his energy. At that point (still holding onto my cane) I tell the dog to "Down." One of two things will happen. If the dog *does* down, go to him *immediately*, bend down and praise him lavishly, then stand up and release him with "get up." Note that you must still hold onto your cane to be prepared when you release him, so do your praising single-handed. Some dogs stop and act a little unsure when you say the "down" command; for them I would repeat the command (just once) to make it clear to them. Later, of course, one command is the limit, but for the dog's first time, I would give him the benefit of the doubt.

The other thing that can happen will be that the dog ignores you and continues running on as though he were stone deaf. Try to hold onto your cane, run him down, get your hands on that line and give him a sharp jerk correction (say nothing—*do not repeat the command*). When the dog goes down, praise lavishly using the word "down" in your praise, keep him there for a few seconds, then release him with the "get up." The reason you keep holding your cane should be obvious to you—your dog will likely dash straight off at the stock upon being released. Have it ready to make him go nice and wide.

Some very tough dogs take quite a bit of correction before they will stop properly. At this stage, therefore, you should go to your dog every time he does go down on command, and praise him. This helps him to not fear your approach—if you went to him only for corrections, he would soon run from you. For a very, very tough dog you may wish to use a two-foot-long piece of soft rubber garden hose. If your dog doesn't stop (and he outruns you for minutes if you try to run him down) you can throw this rubber hose and aim to hit the ground behind the dog. Again, always go to the dog to praise him when he does go down.

It takes *weeks* for the average dog to learn this, so don't be discouraged if your dog doesn't do it all right away. I've had dogs perform fine the first time out while others take months to be really dependable on the stop. Have patience and work, work, work.

Bullenbong Bulli, C.D.X., owned by Gail Ross, shows a good straight approach.

After about fourteen sessions with the dog stopping well and you going to him, discontinue going to him to praise and just verbally praise from a distance each time he stops. Don't forget to release him from each down with the "get up" and also praise him for getting up. If your dog starts popping up before you release him, treat it the same as you would his disobedience; go to him, give a sharp jerk down and *then* praise. You will continue praising him for stopping and getting up for a long time, so get comfortable with it.

If your dog is doing very well you may want to switch from a long line to a short piece of lead on his chain collar. Should the dog require correcting, you will have this short lead to grab onto.

TEACHING THE STEADY APPROACH

Now that your dog is stopping and getting up well, the next thing to teach him is to come up calmly and steadily toward his stock, rather than running in and out. The sequence works like this: Your dog runs around and behind the stock, you stop him, then have him get up, then, on command from you, *he walks straight at the stock, only deviating enough to keep their heads turned toward you.* A good approach is what often makes the difference between a first-rate worker and one that's mediocre.

Watching the heads of the stock, sometimes called "watching the line" (the line being the route the stock is taking) is something all good handlers do, either consciously or not. After all, wherever the heads turn the body must follow! Thus by watching the heads of the stock, you can easily learn the right place to stop your dog.

Let's say your dog has stopped and is in the correct position. You want to be sure you stop him when he is on the far side of the stock from you, so he will then be in a good position to bring the stock to you. When your dog approaches the "top" (the far side of the stock from you), bring your cane up *straight over your head*. If you hold the cane to the side, as you have done, it will cause your dog to "wear" and we're not teaching that here. By holding the cane up you will be signaling him not to flank and wear back and forth.

Once you set your dog down at the top, command him to get up (don't forget praise) and then you should back some distance away from the stock. Your dog will then move toward the stock but if he moves to one side or another, _have him down_, then move yourself so you are in a straight line from the stock. You cannot do this unless you are far enough from the stock that they are not really aware of your presence. Now that you are again back in line with the stock, have your dog get up. As long as he is walking straight toward the stock (a little variation to keep them moving straight to you is okay), let him keep coming on, especially so if he is walking. If he comes on too fast, or wears out to one side stop him instantly. When the stock slows down, have him get up again. This is usually very con-

Letting the dog bring the sheep along behind the handler as she walks is one good way to strengthen a dog's straight approach.

As dog approaches ducks at top of outrun handler holds cane up to avoid mis-cueing dog to over flank.

fusing to the dog the first few times. But by always placing yourself in the position of having the dog bring the stock *without letting him deviate from the straight approach*, he will catch on fast.

Most young dogs come on to their stock too fast, but by periodically stopping the dog each time he starts off fast, you will eventually see him anticipate your stop command so that he slows down. When this happens, allow him to keep going, and he will learn that if he moves up slowly, you will let him work without downing him.

Most dogs without "eye" move too fast and "wear" too much at first. Try to catch the dog as he is first stepping out of line to wear and stop him. This is more effective than stopping him on one side or another. As it's a lot of work for you to then get far enough from the stock, and in a straight line to them (see diagram) but it will pay off in the dog's abilities later.

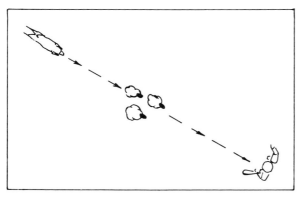

Straight Approach done correctly.

How to correct a bad approach.

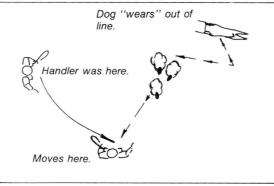

Dog "wears" out of line.

Handler was here.

Moves here.

Few animals can resist a straight approach. Here, trial winner Moss Rogue moves in while the sheep hesitate, then move away.

If you have a dog with a lot of eye, and he is "sticky" (tends to freeze up rather than move on to his stock), there are some ways to get him moving on. One of the best is to turn the stock back onto him. Let's say you have sent your dog around, and stopped him when he gets to the far side. You then have him get up. He may or may not get to his feet at this point, but there he stands, just "eyeing" the stock, ignoring your encouragement to come forward. At this point, many are tempted to call their dog with "Come" but this is disaster, since, in order to obey, your dog should leave the stock and come *straight* to you. Instead, if your dog freezes up, you should stop and then walk *toward* the stock, literally driving them at the dog, all the while repeating "Get up" or "Steady" (use the "Steady" meaning to walk on). I have yet to see a dog lie there while you drive ducks or sheep right over the top of him. Usually at some point when the stock gets very close, the dog will get up and move. When he does, praise lavishly, and use the words "Get up" in your praise. This exercise takes several days of practice before the dog has learned it.

Another way to get the dog to come on is to simply walk farther and farther away. Some dogs will play out all your patience, but if you keep walking backward far enough, most dogs will eventually get up and move the stock to you.

As your dog is bringing the stock on, you may want to quietly repeat a spoken word such as "Steady" or "Walk on." This should be said with the tone of voice conveying the attitude you want your dog to take—a slow, whispery "Steady" to slow down the dog or keep him slow; a fast, excited "Steady" if your dog is hanging back.

Once your dog is getting the idea, practice sending him around, then *quickly* get way back and keep walking backward so the stock has plenty of room to come forward. The more practice the dog gets, the better he will like it.

A variety of mechanical methods are also available to get a dog to come on to his stock. I earnestly advise you to avoid these except as a *last resort*, since the use of them often makes for a dog that is mechanical. Most trainers who use them do so because they are working with a dog that has little natural ability. We breed dogs to have superior natural style and ability but if we are not careful, we can easily turn around and make them nothing but robots, never utilizing their innate qualities. Nevertheless, I will outline a couple of mechanical methods, but remember that they are to be used *only* on a dog that is a second rate worker.

The most common mechanical aid is to put a line on the dog, and when it refuses to come on, give the line a tug toward you, praising as the dog gets up. Another is to put the line on the dog, and together you both walk at the stock while you repeat the command. I have also seen the use of pulleys and various artificial devices, but these are quite unrealistic since you wouldn't have the time to use them in any real situation. (Can you imagine anyone carrying around various implements to work his dog while doing any *real* work?)

Many novices don't know how to recognize their dog's natural abilities. Keep this in mind before you condemn your dog for "failing" when all he might need is a little more time and work. Your dog's natural talent is like a little flower bud that grows with nurturing.

TEACHING THE FLANKING COMMANDS

By now your dog will go around stock, stop, get up, and bring them to you. If he is not able to do these things, do not proceed with teaching the flanking commands *unless* your dog is "hyper-soft." By this I mean he seems very discouraged about the stop (enough so you feel he may lose all interest in working if you continue to practice it). If so, then by all means *do* start teaching the flanking commands as this will increase the dog's interest a hundredfold since it is a fun, easy lesson for both of you.

You should be working your dog in an open space, without fences and big enough that you can move around freely. A good one-half-acre for ducks and at least a full square or circular acre for sheep (preferably more).

You have already noticed that the dog always runs to the opposite side of the flock to balance you; he wants to always keep the flock between you and him. If you walk around the outside of the flock, to your right for instance, the dog runs around (usually to the right) to keep on the far side. Teaching the dog his left from his right is easy. All you need do is walk forward in either direction (with your cane in front of you to keep him from turning back) and label the command or way your dog is running. Walk about two turns around one way, then switch, and walk the other way, doing the same routine.

Teaching the left flanking command. As handler walks to left, dog runs to left to balance off her. (Note tapping of cane to get dog out wide.)

It is important that you always walk forward, as if you were going out for a brisk hike. Do not try to go around the flock like a crab, trying to walk sideways.

As you walk to your left, and as the dog cuts and runs around the flock to his left, you will give the left command, which is "Go bye." I like to repeat this command several times, interspersed with "Good dog!" It's just a drill now, but your dog is listening, nonetheless. After a couple of times your dog will get dizzy, so switch directions, walk forward to the right, and command the dog to "Way to me" or some just say "Away." Every couple of turns change direction. Periodically, stop the dog and then back off and let him bring the stock straight on to you. Then start the going around again.

The big problem novices have at this point is how to keep their left from their right. My best advice is to forget all about *your* left and *your* right, and concentrate on your dog's left or right—*since it is his left and right we are teaching.*

There are two good ways to do this. One is to look at your dog. Is he running to *his* right, or to *his* left? When you concentrate hard on your dog you can see which way is which to him. (Keep in mind that with a gathering dog, these ways will often be exactly opposite to yours, but *don't* concentrate on that or the translation you'll have to work out in your mind will leave you many minutes behind your dog.)

Another way people find easy is to think of clockwise and counter-clockwise. "Go bye" is clockwise, and "Way to me" is counter-clockwise.

Do not for any reason write the commands on your hands and look at your hands to try to recall which way is which. This will confuse you beyond measure, and not help your dog at all.

Many new trainers complain that their dog is so fast, they barely get started and he is on the other side of the flock. If your dog is fast, be faster! (Remember those running shoes?) If you don't run strictly *around* the flock, but also out *at* your dog (making him take the long way around on the extreme outside) you will be able to keep up better. But nothing beats fast footwork. In fact, I have often thought of marketing this lesson as a sure-fire way to lose five pounds. At first you may not be able to do much of this, especially if you are not in great physical shape, but as you condition yourself you will be amazed at how fast you can go.

If you are doing your job with the cane, your dog will not be "sharp flanking" or trying to pull wool or feathers (take a nip). If your dog acts as if he is thinking about these no-no's, be sure to slap the cane *hard* on the ground as he runs, to let him know that you are prepared to protect the stock. It can almost be said that you are, at this point, chasing him out with your cane as he runs around the flock.

Some people have trouble with positioning themselves so their dog doesn't flash in and nip as he goes around. A great deal depends on speed, but if you aim your cane to tap the ground parallel to your dog's rump as he is running, you will do well. Don't ever try to reach over the flock with your cane to protect them. This doesn't work and it allows the dog to get too close. Instead, walk out *at the dog* as he goes around the flock.

After two weeks of frequent drill, your dog will have a hazy idea of left and right, but will not know the commands well. Up until now everything about this lesson has been positive. Now you will teach him that going the wrong way *is* wrong, and you will use your voice to correct him if he runs the wrong way. In teaching this, you will simultaneously be teaching your dog another valuable lesson—how to take the stock off the fence properly.

Set your dog down behind you and then walk closer to your stock, which you have (yourself) herded to a preferably straight fenceline. Hold your cane on the side you *don't* want your dog to go to, then command him to go the "free" way with your usual "Go bye" or "Away." If he tries to run the wrong way, say "No" and block him with your cane. When he turns to run the correct way, praise lavishly and repeat the command with the praise. Let him go all the way to the far side of the flock (near the fence) and bring them out toward you. At first he may overshoot, swinging too far over to the other side. If he does, don't give him the other flanking command, just let him straighten himself out. You may want to encourage this with "Steady." Sometimes the inexperienced dog will be afraid to go in next to the fence, and you may have to open up a thin area next to the fence for him before he will go in close. This is okay at first; you want to build up his confidence.

Working next to the fence. Note position of handler and cane, ready to block dog if it goes the wrong way.

Occasionally a dog will flash through the middle of the flock when asked to go next to the fence. This, too, is lack of confidence. Again, open up a hole between the flock and the fence and send him through.

Some dogs "dive bomb" the flock in this situation, biting and acting crazy. This is most often found in dogs that have not been thoroughly trained in the early lessons, to keep out wide and off the stock. Occasionally this wild behavior indicates a lack of confidence. If your dog does this, I suggest you back up in your lessons and make *sure* your dog understands that biting without permission is bad, and that he runs good and wide. A dog that has been spoiled by an over-indulgent owner, or one that has been allowed to chase stock from a young age, are usually the ones that react this way.

Another way to test your dog and practice on the left and right is to start "redirects." What you will do is stop walking around in a circle with your dog as he goes around the stock, and start standing still, holding your cane straight up (so as not to cue him). If your dog starts to go the wrong way, tell him "No" as many times as it takes to stop him short. When he takes even one step in the correct direction, really praise and repeat the command. Some dogs just don't stop running because you say "No, no." For these you may want to try having the dog lie down. Then repeat the original command and if the dog starts even one stop in the desired direction, really praise! If he goes the wrong way, say "No" again, and if he doesn't pause, set him down again, and so on. Most dogs will pause if you say "No" in a tone that indicates you mean it. This gives you a chance to repeat the command so he can perform it correctly.

Jamaica Spinner, C.D.X., T.D., Belgian Tervuren owned by Janice Turner, bringing sheep out to her mistress.

Using the cane to re-direct the dog.

Directions take awhile for the dog to learn, and you should be sure *you* are clear on them too, so you don't punish your dog for doing something wrong when he really is doing it correctly. If you find yourself getting confused, say nothing until you collect your thoughts. It's better than telling the dog the wrong direction or the wrong words for it, and getting him truly mixed up.

It's difficult for dogs to learn left from right, and if you find yourself getting impatient, remember that as a child it probably took you a long time too. In fact, it has probably taken you a good long time to know *your dog's* left from his right.

8
Starting Short Outruns

Starting the outrun is great fun and gives most dogs a chance to let off some steam. Most herding breeds love to dazzle people with their speed so they take to this like a duck to water. The one exception may be the dog who has had a *lot* of obedience training. He should not be forced into this phase before he shows that he can work without worrying about what you are thinking.

Several commands are used to teach the outrun: The stop ("Down") with no release until told; the left and right flanking commands; the "Steady" or straight approach; and your cane work. Look carefully at the illustrations. Note the positions of the handler and cane at different points during this exercise. It is important that you learn these since the outrun is the single greatest *practical* piece of work your dog will ever do. A dog with a good outrun can save you hours of labor and in trials a judge often forms his initial impression of a dog during the outrun, lift and fetch.

Place the dog several feet behind you. He should be *at least* a cane's distance away, but I prefer to make it more like 15 feet or even more. You have settled your flock and they are preferably standing (or moving slowly) about 40-100 feet from you (or more if your dog is running very wide). Place your cane on the side you *don't* want your dog to run. Turn and face him, if you haven't already. Now give the command for that direction, and *as your dog steps out that way* step out yourself in that same direction, dragging the cane out and walking *at* your dog to force him in a very wide semicircle. When you can see that his outrun is okay, drop back to *your original position*

Proper set up for dog's right hand outrun, in beginning lessons.

Teaching "get back" or "back" with cane by walking *at* the dog as he runs around the stock (to right out of photo).

Running *toward* the dog to force him wider as he gets started on short outrun.

More advanced set-up for right outrun - note handler walking out with cane to force dog out wider. Dog has just been given right directional command, and is coming fast as he passes around *behind* handler.

(when the dog first ran out), then stop the dog at the top of his outrun (on the far side), tell him to get up, and then "Steady," (bring them to you). Always let the dog complete the lift and fetch part of each outrun; he will keep interested that way.

At first you are standing directly parallel to the dog, and both you and your dog are parallel to the stock. (See photos.) If your dog tries to run the wrong way, say "No" and if he tries to keep going, stop him and then set up your outrun from that point. DON'T CALL THE DOG BACK. Use of the cane is also helpful in turning a dog from going in the wrong direction. Slap it hard on the ground to turn him around and get him running in the opposite direction.

INCREASING THE DISTANCE

After many weeks, when you feel your dog is doing these short outruns well, it is time to increase the distance and start to set him up to go wider. You should always do these outruns out in the open away from fences or other possible obstructions. The widest part of the dog's outrun should be the far side of the stock (the top).

Start walking, ever so *gradually*, out a few steps the *way you want the dog to run* as he is lying there waiting for the command to go (see photos). This way the dog has to pass around you and you have a head start on getting him out. If your dog tries to run directly up the middle of the stock, yell (yes, I mean *yell*) "*No!*" in your most frightening voice. Stop the dog before he gets up the field. Go to him, and set up the outrun from that point again. *Don't call him back.*

Some dogs worry about getting up to the left or right commands without the "Get up" first. For them you may want to tell them to get up right before the direction command. Most dogs get over this once they learn what fun the outruns are. With a few dogs I just stand there looking at them as they lie there. Then I repeat the direction command, the the minute they act like they are stirring, I praise them. By "setting up" the outrun this way you are also cueing the dog that an outrun is about to happen. This makes him very happy and excited, and he will tend to run faster on his outrun—just what you want.

Eventually, you will be able to walk a good distance out to one side or the other to send your dog and he will pass around behind you, swinging wide, to gather. Never rush these important lessons.

Some dogs can go quite far on their first try, but more often, they need to start in fairly close to the flock. Over weeks and months, foot by foot, you should increase the distance they can handle. If at any time your dog starts to run in too close, cross over, charge up the middle, or "cut off" the top of his outrun so that he's flanking in sharp on the flock, reduce the distance and go back to working more on basics. Take plenty of time, and get each step down pat before proceeding.

Most novice trainers are in a big hurry to try outruns of vast distances, but this temptation can ruin your dog's future as an effective worker. Once a dog learns that he can cut in, he will try it whenever he thinks you can't stop him. I must caution you again to go slowly—remember, increase by feet rather than by yards or acres.

THE "PEAR-SHAPED" OUTRUN

Up until now the outrun has been a semicircular shape, but the pear-shaped is well liked in many trial circles. A word of caution—most of the herding breeds run in close. Teach the pear-shaped outrun *only* if your dog runs naturally wide, and you plan to compete in trials. If you are planning to do only ranch work, just teach the semicircle. The semicircular outrun is more apt to gather your *whole* flock in a real range situation. A dog does save energy in a pear-shaped outrun, but he also cuts off some of the field, and if you have brush or hills where sheep can hide, the dog is more apt to bring in only the sheep he sees and not look for any others that may be hiding. This is a subject of much debate at trials, and there are some strong feelings toward each kind of outrun.

To teach the pear-shaped outrun, put the dog on a down (as with the semicircle), set your flock down the field a bit, and turn and face the dog. Instead of being fairly close to the dog, you should be about halfway to the flock. This way your dog gets up on command, takes the direction, but is more or less running straight until he hits your position, at which time you force him out wide to the side you direct. The actual outrun looks like a pear, with the small part at the start and the big part at the top.

One often hears of various ways "guaranteed" to make your dog run wider on his outrun. Most aren't effective but one method that has *occasionally* worked is to work the dog in a bigger area with rather wild, fast-moving stock. Another possibility is to set up a situation where some sheep are hidden from the dog's view (i.e., in bushes) and are released just as the dog is starting to go past them. Sometimes the shock that he could have missed some strays will cause a dog to run wider so he can see the whole field. Some dogs (especially the smart ones) learn that in a big area on very wild stock they have to keep out or they lose the flock.

There is no substitute for long weeks of short practices, over and over, with enthusiastic praise when the dog performs correctly. A good outrun may take a long time to develop, or it may be natural to your dog. My observation is that few breeds have truly natural outruns. The ones most apt to have them are Border Collies, some Kelpies and Beardies, or Canaans.

LENGTHENING OUTRUNS

Now that your dog is doing good, wide, short outruns, start to increase the distance very slowly. One day you might send him 100 yards, and the next day 101 yards. Don't send him 100 yards one day and 300 the next! Patience is the key.

A big, wide open area is essential to develop a good outrun. You cannot teach a wide outrun in small, confined areas. If you are working sheep, now is the time to get out into a bigger pasture; if you're working ducks, get out to a big field, Little League field or park.

Border Collie running wide left at great distance. Note sheep at top of photo.

At first, try to work in an area free of obstacles such as piles of wood, barns and outbuildings, brush, etc. These can be introduced later so the dog easily accepts running around or over them. In the learning stages, he's just trying to understand what you want.

If your sheep or ducks are very wild and tend to run all over the place while you are trying to get set up for your outrun, you may wish to reduce the distance (to compensate for the amount of distance they will gain before you can send the dog) or get milder stock for the time being. If your stock drifts badly to one side or another, change your set-up to offset this. For instance, let's suppose you left your flock in the center of the field and walked downfield to do a left-hand outrun with your dog. In the meantime, the flock drifted badly to the left side, perhaps next to a fence or outbuilding. In this case, the smart thing to do would be to re-set your dog and yourself and send him to the right. *Always send the dog to the most open end for his outrun.*

Each time you let your dog bring the flock in to you after an outrun, he feels a sense of accomplishment and learns that he is there for a definite purpose; his goal is to bring the flock to you. Later he will learn that he can do more than this, but for now this is pretty heady stuff to him.

Remember, some dogs will take as long as a year to get a good, long outrun. Don't push too hard.

RE-DIRECTING ON THE OUTRUN

There are early and easy re-directs, and there are later, harder ones. In the early re-directs the dog was learning how to distinguish left from right, and how to take the command *regardless of your position.* But as your outruns get longer and longer, you will need to direct the dog inches or feet to the sides, and after he has gone just far enough to turn the flock's heads back toward you, you can stop the dog or steady him on. Here he will be taking the commands but they will still be close to what he wants to do.

Start letting the flock drift out of line by stopping your dog and keeping him down longer than you ordinarily would. When the flock drifts to one side, use the flanking command to get the dog out there to turn them, then stop him once the stock is coming back in the desired straight line to you. Don't encourage the dog to take them out of line himself, rather, let the stock drift out of line by themselves, then have the dog straighten them out. This way he will learn to always bring them to you in a straight line.

Another form of re-directing is to send the dog back after something. Ideally, there should not be strays but if there are, you should stop the dog, then try to get his attention with "Look back." This is the one and only time it might be okay to point. However, most dogs will have no idea what you're after, and will continue along their way. You may have to stop the dog, walk up to him, take him by the collar and turn him around, letting him go only when you are certain he has spotted the strays. Keep telling him "Look back."

It's a good idea to set up this "strays" situation. Your dog is working the flock but you have separated one or a few and hidden them. Another approach is to set the dog down, walk among the flock yourself, separate some of them and drive them away a bit. In either case, when the stage has been set, alert the dog by telling him to "Look back."

Any time your dog returns some strays, *the minute their heads turn back to the flock set the dog down.* The bodies of the sheep or ducks will follow their heads; when they turn back to the flock the dog has won. Letting a dog stampede stock back or run them through the flock is very bad. You want your dog to learn to bring strays back calmly and quietly, with little fuss. Once you and your dog have planted the idea in the minds of the animals that in order to get away from the dog they must return to the flock, your problems are solved.

The most difficult form of re-directing is to send the dog back after another group or flock, completely hidden from him. This takes trust from your dog, and I usually recommend that the dog be familiar with "running on the blind" (going after stock he can't see) before you do this.

RUNNING ON THE BLIND

A practical ranch dog that can find stock which is not in plain view is a wonderful asset. In the long run, he will save his master a lot of time and steps. *Never* try to teach a young, untrained or inexper-

Heavily wooded or brushy country like this are areas where a dog "running on the blind" is most useful.

ienced dog to run on the blind. In fact, many wait until their dog has been working six months to a year before they start this exercise, and surely the deciding criteria must be that your dog is doing very good *long* outruns in the proper way before you should even think about teaching running on the blind.

To start, deliberately set up a situation for the dog. Put a flock in a pasture of very high weeds, cornstalks, or very brushy land, then walk back and get your dog. On the first lesson, you may want to let him see you put the sheep out there, even though they are gone from his sight by the time you return. Next, set him up for his usual outrun. If he looks confused, tries to run round in a circle or otherwise looks like he's in trouble, walk closer to the sheep and send him again. If he acts confused, walk even closer.

I always use "Look back" with a directional command when using a dog to run on the blind, as the "Look back" (from his earlier lesson) helps him to understand that something is hiding—something he can't see out there.

Each time you practice running on the blind, your dog should be better at it. Always make sure he DOES find the flock and that he DOES bring them in to you each and every time; success is a great confidence builder. On the other hand, even one failure will set him back incredibly far. Take the time and do it right.

Eventually, your dog will get familiar with the layout of your land and the regular places he works, so if you have more than one area suitable for this lesson, make use of those. Challenge him with variety so he will be able to handle running on the blind in the "real world"—out on the range. In this situation you may find that the dog loses a bit of polish and elegance when he is called upon to run on the blind. My feeling is that if it works, it's okay, but try to prevent any *major* faults such as crossing over on his cast (outrun), grabbing hold or pulling wool, etc. I usually find that a dog will get back his refinement after he's secure about what he's doing.

Lucky and Foxy, McNabs, getting ducks out of the pond to bring to the barn.

SOME GENERAL THINGS TO THINK ABOUT

Since you have gone this far with your dog, now is the time to start modifying a bit of what you are doing.

- First, begin to switch over to whistled commands in earnest. Whistle, then give the verbal command. Keep practicing day after day; the dog will learn to adapt to the whistle.

- Also, if he has been stopping well, it is no longer necessary for him to lie down each time you stop him. If he wants to stand or sit, these are both okay. I let a dog stand all he wants until the first time he just plain doesn't stop when told; then I make him lie down. Each time he doesn't stop (stand) but keeps on running, I make him lie all the way down. The dog gets the message fast.

- Although I haven't expressly said so, by the time you are doing long outruns you should have no line whatsoever on your dog. You may, however, wish to keep him working in the chain collar for a while, or go back to it if the dog is slow to stop.

- If you are having specific problems, look in the problems section of this book and try to correct them before they become bad habits.

- When your dog is running wide on his own, you may dispense with the cane. However, if he starts to run in close, bring the cane back out.

- Remember to *gradually* work anything new or unusual (new stock, new place, you on horseback,) into the dog's repertoire.

- *If your dog is very soft* I always recommend working him in as many new places as possible, right from the start. These dogs easily become dependent, so to break any tendencies of that nature I give the dog new challenges each day. Soft dogs become accustomed to routine and may fall apart when asked to vary it with something new.

9

Penning

Introduce the penning lesson when your dog is stopping well, knows his left and right, *and re-directs well in close*. You could start the pen earlier, but penning is a difficult and complex subject. If you want to learn to pen properly, and always get it right, you would be very wise to wait until your dog is well along in his training.

I like to use a freestanding pen right from the start; not the kind built into a wall or fenceline. (This is one of the greatest shortcomings of the current A.S.C.A. trial course—the pen is set into a fenceline and the animals simply run in. It's impossible to tell what kind of work the dogs can do at this crucial phase.) For ducks, a wire, freestanding exercise pen (available from dog supply outlets and at dog shows) is great. For sheep, you can easily put together four panels (the kind most shepherds have on hand to move sheep around in close spaces) and tie them with rope or wire so they will stand by themselves. Leave one side loose so it can swing out.

Using a freestanding pen is far preferable to using another kind, since your dog develops the concept of taking the stock *straight in* and guarding his movements so that the stock doesn't split and run all over and around the pen. In classes I have worked with Aussies and their owners who trained right from the start on a pen built into a fenceline. These dogs are, without exception, sloppy in their work at the pen. They are constantly prone to lose the stock around the pen, not because they aren't good dogs, but because they were not correctly trained about penning. Many did extremely well after being taught the proper penning techniques.

The following are some rules of penning:

- NEVER try to *run* stock into a pen. Let them investigate the pen opening and saunter in. Ease them in inch-by-inch but don't try to force them in with a wild charge.

- ALWAYS have the dog bring the stock to the pen on his strongest side (the side that is facing you).

- DON'T have the dog bring the stock around *behind you* at the pen. Have him bring them out and then in facing you, from the side facing the opening of the pen.

- DON'T allow your dog to over-flank at the pen. Move him inches left or right and make him be cautious. Over-flanking always loses the sheep around the pen sides.

- DON'T *you* move around at the pen; to do so only scares the stock and is often enough to keep them away. By holding still you also have the effect of alerting the dog as to what's about to take place. After a few times, he *knows* that when you take up your position, you and he will be going for the penning. (Note: In Britain it is considered very bad form if the handler doesn't help the dog pen the sheep by use of the cane and sometimes by edging inward on that far side. But in some American trials too much help from the handler is frowned upon. At your own ranch or home you should help the dog as much as is sensible, but at trials know what the rules are and act accordingly.

- DON'T use sharp words or any whistling at the pen. Use very low, gentle voice tones instead. A hiss, rather than a whistle, is a good way to stop the dog at the pen.

To practice the pen, have your dog bring the stock to within about 100 feet of the pen. Stop him and let the stock settle. Now go to your pen and open the gate outward to its widest point. In order to keep

Proper position
for penning (wire
mesh pen used
here for ducks).
Note strong
position of dog as
he brings ducks
in to handler.

The heads of the
stock must be
facing *into* the
pen before you
start to close your
gate.

Ch. Harvest's Tear's Pride N Joy, S.T.D., owned by Kathy Davis. Teaching the
dog to stop at the gate is sometimes helpful.

Never try to run sheep into a pen or chute. Ease them in inch-by-inch and let them see that the enclosure is their only option. Keeping the dog on his feet increases his powerful position.

yourself from walking around, hold onto the side of the gate, or to a rope tied to the gate. Stand firm. Extend your cane slowly and gently to your open side (see photos) to block that side. Now have your dog *slowly* walk the stock up, a few feet at a time. Any time the stock moves out of a very slow walk, stop your dog. Convey to him by your posture and "stage-whisper" voice that something is happening here that requires his utmost concentration. If the stock are headed for the opening of the pen but want to stop and look at the pen, let them do so for a moment. They must have the chance to contemplate their options. The opening of the pen may seem like a trap to them, but they will go in if they are not terrorized. If they become frightened, they will NEVER go into a "trap." (There is an old saying among shepherds that sheep on the run, do so "blind." That is, they get crazy and will even run off cliffs. In their panic, all mental processes shut down.)

As the stock edges nearer to the pen, keep your dog moving only enough to turn the heads of the stock into the pen opening. Try to keep him on his feet, though—a lot of popping up and down can be startling to stock at the pen. Do not lose your temper, or wave your cane, speak loudly or do anything that might scare off the stock. A student of mine suggested that penning was like trying to catch a wild sparrow in a cage. Use that same caution, and your attitude will be correct.

When the stock gets to the opening, try to have the dog ease them in from his side, as you slowly begin to close the gate from your side. You and he are like two sides of a vise. Don't start to close the gate until all the heads of the stock are pointed into the pen. Should an animal cut back and try to get out, have your dog quickly turn it. Stop him when the head of the animal is again pointed into the pen.

What if the stock breaks and runs around the pen as they approach? This is most often caused by the dog moving too fast (thus the stock is moving too fast), or by the dog working too close; often both at once. A dog that is working too close at the pen creates a hit and miss situation—if the animals feel like going in, they go; if not, the dog just chases them around and around. If your dog is very loose-eyed, you have an extra problem.

Having very little or no eye can be a pleasure in some circumstances, but at the pen you have to steady the loose-eyed dog some. Generally, the strong-eyed dog is easier to get to concentrate and move catlike slowly up, but the loose-eyed dog tends to over-flank in this situation. It takes a lot of practice to get the loose-eyed dog in the habit of stopping on a dime and moving inches one way or the other. Most want to go too far, take a few extra steps so they can indulge in this over-flanking, and as a result the stock sways one way, then the next, always just missing the gate of the pen.

Chute on an ASCA course is worked much like a free standing pen. Note calmness of sheep.

If, through your attitude and "stage-whisper" voice, you convey controlled intensity to your dog, even the loose-eyed dog will begin to show more caution and concentration.

If your dog should single one animal off at the pen, let him flank out super wide to turn it back. NEVER try to pen stock one at a time. If the animals split, gather them all up, move them a bit away from the pen, then have the dog bring them in to you at the gate.

Some dogs do get more excited than we would like and if the stock faces them at the pen gate they are inclined to lose their tempers. If your stock is all set in the mouth of the pen, but is facing outward and is looking at your dog, *don't* let him bite. Convey by a slow, easy tone of voice that you want him to "Steady" and bring him up step-by-step. Having the dog nip at the wrong time can cause the sheep to bolt and run, making it twice as hard to pen them on the next try.

Ch. Slash V Easy Jet, C.D., S.T.D., moving sheep easily into a pen. Jet is an Aussie.

10
Teaching a Dog to Grip

When starting your dog, make every effort to get stock that won't fight him, even if you have to resort to ducks. At some point, however, your dog will have to face stock that will fight him, or at least turn and challenge his authority. You will want him to be prepared and know how to react without getting hurt or losing his head and tearing up the stock. It's best to teach this as a lesson instead of waiting until you've got some aggressive rams bearing down on your dog.

Some dogs are very confident; some are not. Also, some are strong-eyed while other are loose-eyed. The strong-eyed dog creeps up to within a certain radius of the stock, and if the animals turn and face him, the dog may charge in and grip naturally. This is rarely a problem with a loose-eyed dog—he will be more inclined to walk right up to an aggressive old ewe and even touch noses with her, often only gripping if the ewe attacks first. It is much easier to get a loose-eyed dog to come up straight in the face of a challenge from stock than it is a very strong-eyed dog.

The very assertive, confident dog is keen to nip and you may have already spent some time teaching him not to do so whenever he felt like it. You *must* have him broken of spontaneous tendencies to pull wool, etc. before you can go back and teach him to nip. Set up a situation where you catch a single sheep from the flock and back her into a corner of fence, with her head facing OUT toward the field. Have your dog on a down and *make him stay down until told otherwise.* When you are set (hold the sheep around the lower neck or shoulder), have your dog come up. Some dogs will dive in just at the sight of you holding this sheep (the dog is eager to help his pack leader catch the prey). If he comes up fast, use your command to grip (some say "Hit 'em" while others prefer a low hiss). If, on the other hand, he hangs back and needs to be encouraged to come up and nip the sheep's face, struggle with the sheep a bit, and touch it lightly on the nose. This usually will prompt the dog to come in. When the dog gets close, use the low hiss or "Hit 'em" spoken in a very excited tone of voice.

After the dog has come up and nipped, release the sheep to go back to the flock, set the dog *immediately down*, and tell him "That's enough" or whatever you have chosen to mean "no more nipping." The down is important, since otherwise the dog will run around the single sheep and head it back to you, or jump on it and bite it.

With the dog that lacks confidence, nothing has a more positive effect than teaching him to nip on command. This dog can be easily bullied by sheep, who may sense the dog's lack of confidence and take shameless advantage. Any dog may lack confidence, but it seems to be more common in the smaller breeds that look like easy targets to aggressive sheep.

In training this type of dog to grip, use a rather small sheep or even an older lamb. Catch and hold it in the corner and follow the instructions given above. Many of these dogs won't nip, but will come up and bark, click their teeth, bump with their noses, and use ANYTHING that is an assertive move. Remember to make a big fuss over *any* kind of assertiveness, no matter how comical it may be. *Let the dog know how thrilled you are* when he stands up to the sheep. Most of these dogs want to make you happy, and if they see that you're pleased over this mildly aggressive move, they will gain in confidence. *Take great care* to not let the sheep run over the dog when you turn it loose.

With this milder type of dog, gradually work up to large sheep. At first he may come up and bark, then, after days of practice, he will bump with his nose, and then, weeks later, get up the courage to nip. Don't immediately put him on the most aggressive ram you have that will then squish the poor little dog into the dirt. If you started with a lamb, work up to a grown ewe, then a little larger ewe and finally, when your dog is really into it (usually after months), you can put him on the more aggressive stock. You may find this gradual building up of confidence tedious, but it will pay off for years to come.

It is important to teach a dog to defend himself—all sheep are *not* docile! Here, a young Border Collie is attacked by an aggressive ewe. Teaching a dog to grip can eliminate this problem.

Nothing is more awful than the alternative—a dog that cuts and runs at the slightest aggressive move by your sheep!

Two more points: do not use the same sheep each time you practice gripping; use a different sheep each time. Also, be careful of where your hands are, as some dogs will run up blindly and may accidentally nip at your hand as well as the sheep.

What if your dog comes in too strong, latches onto a sheep and won't let go? There are two things you can do:

1) you can reach out with your hand as the dog is holding on (you are still holding onto the sheep, or someone else is holding it) and slap the dog under the jaw, hard, while saying, "That's enough!", or

2) you can put the dog on a chain collar with a sturdy leather lead attached. When the dog comes up and grabs and won't let go, reach to the dog and give it a *sharp* jerk off the sheep and repeat "That's enough!"

Over a period of time, back way from the sheep and turn it to face the dog. Still standing close by, give the dog that command to "Hit it," or a hiss. As time goes by, you should be able to back off further and further, and encourage your dog from more distance. Eventually your goal is to be able to have your dog nip on command from any distance when the sheep directly challenge him.

ASCH Apache Tears of Timberline, U.D., A.T.D., an Aussie owned by Nick Davis, stands up to a challenge from a stubborn ewe.

11

Understanding and Preparing for the Drive

There are as many theories on training the drive as there are trainers. I am going to offer you an approach that has worked with a majority of my students and with my own dogs. There is no one correct approach to driving, but I think that you, as a beginning trainer, will find this method far easier and more logical than some others.

The greatest difference of opinion is over *when* to start the drive. Many trainers feel the dog should be well schooled in the basics of gathering before he drives, while others start the drive almost immediately, teaching it at the same time as the gather. Some teach the drive before the dog even knows flanking commands. It is wise to keep in mind that most of those who subscribe to the latter theories (and there are many professional trainers who don't) are, by and large, men who have been training for many, many years, and have "seen it all." They usually also have the facilities to accommodate any type of training lesson, something the novice will find very hard to match. I have *never* seen a novice successfully train for the fetch and the drive at the same time, not ever, and I have seen a great many potentially good dogs wrecked by this sort of training. The novice trainer does not have the vast experience to spot when things are going wrong. Therefore, the novice continues on, adding problem onto problem, until it is an impossible thing to correct. Don't try to convince yourself that *you* are above all that and won't make those mistakes. All beginners make mistakes, even advanced trainers do...they just don't make the same ones!

To know if your dog is ready for the drive, ask yourself these questions:

1. Can my dog do a good 200 to 300-yard outrun properly?

2. Does my dog know his flanking commands (directions) very well?

3. Does my dog re-direct well?

If the answer is "Yes" to all three questions, you are ready to proceed to the drive.

PARALLEL DRIVE ALONG A FENCE

The first step in teaching the drive is the *parallel drive along a fence*. Using rather docile stock, set them along a long, straight fence. Place your dog on a down or stop behind them (don't send him out there, walk up and *place* him there). Have your dog get up and "Steady" onto the stock. You remain beside the stock on the outside, opposite the fence. If the dog tries to flank toward the fence (to push the stock out to you) stop him immediately, and if he has moved out of the straight line, use your left or right command to bring him into line. (Some people like to teach the drive using slightly different commands. I do this, but I don't advise everyone to do so. For some dogs, it is less confusing to them to have drive words *and* gather words; but for others, learning multiple commands is just too hard.)

Your goal is to have the dog push the stock down the fenceline as *you walk parallel to the stock*. Don't get ahead of them and don't get very far behind, stay out to the side, steadying that side of the flock. Walk along to keep up, keeping the dog behind them (see photos). Don't use the cane too much here, only if you must block the dog. Any time your dog deviates and tries to run the stock at you, stop him, using the command "Steady." Always stop the dog if he tries to cut around in front of you. You must be on your toes here, since the dog *will* be trying to get around, and you will be trying to keep him behind the stock.

If your dog should get past you and start to bring the stock out to you, don't yell at him, just set him down, call him off, and leave him on a down farther away while you go back and place the stock on the fence. At this stage, don't have the dog do it. Repeat the lesson, with you placing the dog behing the stock and asking him to "Steady." When you have reached the end of the fenceline, stop the dog, turn the stock back the other way *yourself,* and continue having the dog "Steady," driving down the other way along the fence, as you walk parallel to the stock. Do the same when you reach the end of the fenceline that way, and repeat the entire lesson once again.

You might think it strange that *you are doing all this placing, but you will only be doing it the first few times. At this point, you don't want to give your dog the idea that he can mix up these two types of work—driving and gathering. It is VERY IMPORTANT that your dog understand that gathering and driving are two different* things. A dog that has become confused about this tends to run around and turn back stock on his drive, or not go all the way around on his gather. Sometimes he will even stop at some point and take the stock *away.*

Parallel drive along a fence.

- 99 -

In order to make it very clear to your dog what the differences are, plan your lesson so that you have a "Gather time" and a "Drive time." The following is the lesson plan which I use for all the drive training:

- Start with outrun, lift and fetch, left side.
- At completion of fetch, let stock go and do outrun, lift and fetch, right side.
- Do another left-hand outrun. Do another right-hand outrun, each time letting the dog complete his lift and fetch to you.
- Call dog off, set up for a drive. Practice driving for about 15 minutes.
- Call dog off, let stock go, finish up with one left outrun and one right outrun, letting dog complete lifts and fetches.

Sometimes it's helpful to let the dog break for a few minutes in between fetching and driving. IT IS IMPORTANT FOR NOW THAT YOU CALL OFF THE DOG BEFORE MAKING THE SWITCH FROM FETCHING TO DRIVING AND VICE VERSA. Later on, it will be less important, for your dog will know what you want. But at first, make it clear that these are very different lessons.

Ch. Slash V Eash Jet, C.D., S.T.D., doing a parallel drive along the fence with owner Doug Bailey.

Practice the parallel drive until you are sure your dog understands and is taking his flanking commands well. He should no longer be fighting you about trying to slip around the stock and bring them off the fence. When he has fully accomplished this stage, it is time for the parallel drive in the open.

PARALLEL DRIVE IN THE OPEN

This is the same thing you've been doing, but instead of having the fence to steady one side of the flock, you are now taking them into the open. You will continue to walk parallel to the flock, as your dog moves them from behind. Be aware that this is your dog's big chance to get around the sheep before you can stop him, so be quick to use that stop before he gets more than a few feet out of line. (Carefully examine the driving series photos for the correct positions.) Drive the flock down the field in this fashion, and then turn them and drive them the other way. At this point, let *your dog* turn them, but be quick to stop him before he gets all the way around. You'll know when to stop him by watching the heads of the flock. *When their heads turn the*

Parallel drive in the open. Handler stays parallel to the sheep as dog drives forward.

direction you want, stop your dog. Then walk parallel to the flock the other way as the dog drives from behind.

If this sounds confusing, it isn't. You are taking the flock one way down the field, then turning them and bringing them back, all the while using the elements of the parallel drive. Practice this often, but don't neglect your outruns, lifts and fetches. If you do, the outrun will go to pot.

One day your dog will no longer be fighting you to get around the flock. When that day comes you should start to drop back. Up until now, you have been parallel to the flock. Now you should walk slower, let the flock get a little ahead of you, and allow your dog to take them on ahead. Don't get very far behind, just be content to walk slower. Don't let too much distance get between your position and that of your dog, though you should not be near him.

Gradually, over weeks or months, begin to drop back more, walking slower and slower, and finally walking *very* slowly the other way (backward) as your dog goes forward. At this stage you are ready for the next phase.

Driving. Note that the Aussie is driving away steadily and the sheep are calm and well grouped. ASCH Apache Tears of Timberline, A.S.U.D., A.T.D., owned by Nick Davis.

THE STRAIGHT DRIVE AWAY

Many trainers are impatient to get to this point and don't spend enough time on the steps preceding it. Dogs that are urged into a straight line drive too soon often fight their masters for control forever. Don't fall into this trap. Take your time, be persistent, practice, and really praise your dog as he accomplishes each lesson.

You have been dropping back farther and farther, and now you will get to a point where you just stand while your dog drives on ahead, taking his commands for left, right, stop and steady. Since most dogs get the flanking commands well on the drive before they come straight onto the stock with much power, make sure your flock will move freely for him at this point. After he's confident in his drive, you can re-introduce the nip on command if the flock gives him trouble. To put him on rank sheep at this stage is inviting him to break the drive and slip around. If you command him to grip while he's driving he'll be apt to circle first, then nip. Very bad. So for now, use free moving stock. Practice the straight drive away by sighting objects (a tree, old post) and then have your dog drive the stock to this object.

CAUTION: _Never, never_ command your dog to drive the flock away and then, from the drive, command him to go around and fetch them. This is guaranteed to produce a dog that slips around at bad times and brings the stock to you on drives. If you want the flock back, call the dog _all the way off_, back to you, then set him up for an outrun, and send him that way. With a fully trained dog combining these two procedures won't matter, but with a partly trained dog, you must try hard not to confuse him. _Don't_ combine the fetch and the drive for now.

THE CROSS DRIVE

This is the most difficult phase of driving since it demands more skill from you, as a handler, and more precision and obedience from your dog. On the cross drive, your dog will drive across the field, some distance, and parallel to you, but you will be a good distance away (see photos). The dog is out there, virtually on his own, and must rely on your whistled or spoken flanking commands, stops, and steadys to get the flock where you want it. The hard part for you, as the handler will be depth perception. Like gauging the distance between cars when you first learn to drive, gauging distances is something that is learned with cross driving. You will think your sheep are headed for a gate, but will find that you have miscalculated and they are too deep to the other side. Your depth perception has tricked you. The only way to learn it is to do it, over and over. It helps to have a goal (a gate, post, tree) for your dog to drive the flock to.

The cross drive will really test your dog's knowledge of his commands. Many dogs will slip around and fetch (especially when taking the flanking command that will put them on the farther side of the flock from you) if they have been pushed too fast. If at any time you find yourself in a "war of wills" with your dog, back up and return to parallel drives and short, straight drives.

Cross-drive. Dog drives sheep across on a parallel to handler. Handler remains in one spot.

Imp. Bullenbong Bulli, C.D.X., on his cross drive. Bulli is owned by Gail Boss.

Drive training represents a committment from you; once you start it, you *must* continue on. A good driving dog cannot be trained in a session one month here, and a session a few months later. You must work the dog often and put in lots of time and practice to develop the skills necessary for a good driving dog.

TEACHING THE SHEDDING

Shedding is a fun thing to teach, but should never be attempted with a young, inexperienced dog. To teach it too soon can create a problem dog who splits sheep when you don't want him to.

To be honest, I don't know a lot of handlers who *use* shedding in real-life situations the way it's done at trials. I am told that in Britain it is still used, but we don't use it very much here in America. But in most of the bigger trials patterned after the British trials, there is a "shed" and sometimes, two.

Shedding is singling off one sheep or a number of sheep, and holding them away from the flock for the shepherd to catch (i.e., for doctoring, help in lambing). In a trial, the "shed" is conducted in a "shedding ring" that the sheep must be taken to and held in until the dog has made the cut for his sheep. The handler is not allowed to help unduly with his body or cane, but there is, nonetheless, an art to handling the shed. A lot of good trials runs fall apart because the handler makes a mistake at the shedding ring.

The shed should be developed properly on a large flock, preferably of sheep, though, for some fun and laughs, you can use ducks. About fifty head is idea; more if you have them. Twenty-five would be the smallest number I'd recommend at first. Shedding on a big flock is much easier than on a single animal. It also gives the dog a sense that he's doing somthing useful and, therefore, he will learn faster.

Shedding. Handler lets sheep string out with dog on other side poised to come in.

Get the flock into the open and then set your dog down on the far side. Let the flock settle; they should be standing. Slowly walk into the middle, with your goal being to split the flock into two equal groups. Call the dog to "Come in here" as you start to move, encouraging him to come straight to you through the flock. A lot of dogs will dash past and run to gather up the flock. If yours does, you will need to keep after him, and you may need to almost complete the cut yourself before he'll come straight in. Once you have a cut, encourage the dog to drive one group far away from the rest; go with him

Shedding. Sheep are split into two groups as handler calls dog straight in with "come in, here!"

some to give him the idea that it's okay. It also helps if you really have someplace to take this group (a pen, barn, corral). This makes the dog think there's some purpose to it all. For the first few practices, don't use the dog to put the flock back together as this will only reinforce his natural desire to circle and hold them together.

After split, dog drives one group away to another area.

After the dog will come in without hesitation when you start the shed, you can begin to stand still and just use your cane to help the sheep sift and string out. See if your dog will take the initiative and come in, making the cut on his own. If he does, praise him and drive the one section off just as you always do.

Over a period of months, you can reduce the size of the flock until you are down to about ten head. This is a much harder shed. Try splitting it in half for several days or even weeks if your dog finds it too difficult. If an animal looks like it may get past him back to the flock, help him drive it away and hold it out. Let him see that you are partners, that he can count on you.

Eventually, you may work down to five sheep and shedding a single sheep. This is quite a challenge, and my best advice is to try your best not to let the sheep get past the dog. Call him off if it looks like this is going to happen. You want to avoid failures. Once your

Practical shedding. Dog and handler split off a ewe with twins that need medical attention.

dog is able to shed a few head, when you are finished with the shed, you can then send the dog on around to put the flock back together.

In order to avoid problems with shedding, be sure to let the sheep relax and string out. Also, make sure the dog isn't out too wide, or in too close (making the sheep huddle together fearfully). If the dog is _really_ too close the sheep won't settle and stand; instead they mill closely one way and the next, tightly packed. You have to get your dog in the right place at the right time.

Another common problem is that a few hot tempered dogs will grip, especially if the shedded sheep starts to get past them. Be sure your dog understands when and why he should grip, and don't allow it in tense situations like the shed and pen. An even better solution is to teach your dog to grip ONLY ON COMMAND. There is no confusion—he knows he is not to do it until you give the okay.

Dog moves ewe and lambs into a pen where they can be caught and doctored.

The late ASCH Harvest's Sparkling Tears, C.D., A.T.D., owned by Marleen Davis.

12
Trial Work

When your dog is completely trained you may feel very proud of him and want to enter some trials. There are many kinds of trials in the United States with many types of courses, and many types of judging. Before proceeding to what you should do to ready your dog for trials, you should have an overall view of what you will be getting into.

Trials are designed to test the dog in some everyday functions. They are among the most useful and close-to-real-life tests we have for dogs, but, nonetheless, they often fall short of being perfect. A valid criticism of trials is that emphasis is placed on specific things and a "trial dog" may be developed at the expense of the everyday "working" dog. In fact, some of the consistent trials winners are kept only for trials competition and never worked on the range, for fear of wrecking them for trials. Herein lies the weakness in trials, but efforts are constantly being made to improve them, and at the moment they are the best we have.

In America we have two major trials systems—those patterned after the British trials, such as those designed and sponsored by North American Sheepdog Society and American International Border Collie Reg. (A.I.B.C.), and their affiliates, and those of the Australian Shepherd Club of America (A.S.C.A.), which is basically an American invention, unrelated to any trials courses in Australia or Britain.

The basic North American or A.I.B.C. course has a long outrun (200-500 yards), lift and fetch, followed by a straight drive-away through a gate set midway up the field, then a cross drive to a second gate, then back to the handler and finally to the pen. Many of the trials have a "shed," that is, cutting certain sheep or one sheep away and holding it away to the judge's satisfaction (much like the cutting horse holding out a calf). The handler is stationary, standing downfield, all during the dog's outrun, lift, fetch and both drives, and may only move during the pen and shed. Such trials may be judged by a single judge, a panel of judges, or by a "scorekeeper" system where points are given for each panel made. Many affiliates use this same type of course.

The A.S.C.A. system in America is unique, and because it has not worked closely with either British or Australian systems, it is quite different from any other course (something Border Collie handlers almost universally think is a giant mistake). Because so little was known about the Australian Shepherd's working abilities in the beginning of this Club, the course was not designed to fully test what Aussie owners know their dogs can do. Therefore, A.S.C.A. made some mistakes in this course, but plans are being made to revise the course somewhat. By the time you read this, those changes may have been implemented.

Bess, trials winning Border Collie owned by the author, working flighty sheep in an open trial. Patience is essential with trial sheep!

The course starts with a pen, attached to a fence, from which the dog takes the stock and drives down a fenceline to the first gate, thence through the second gate, attached to a fence, and into the middle where the dog must negotiate the stock through a mock "chute" and from there, back to the pen. There is no outrun and no clear driveaway that isn't aided by a fenceline, and the handler is free to walk about the course—the extent of which is determined by the class the dog is in. A.S.C.A. trials are judged either by one judge or a panel of judges.

In addition to these major systems, there are little local sheep-dog clubs that often sponsor trials, and some have their own trials courses, too numerous to outline in detail. Most are based on a North American or modified North American course, and are often held in conjunction with local fairs and sheep sales.

There are basically two kinds of judges in trials—the ones who like to see the dog do a lot of the work on his own, and the ones who like to see a dog controlled every step of the way. ALL have one thing in common—a good judge always evaluates a dog by his *effect on the flock*. If the dog has a positive effect on the flock, that is the dog the judges will most often prefer. This is not to say there are judges who will confuse you, and a few, frankly, probably shouldn't be judging at all. But these are a minority; most judges try very hard to judge correctly and impartially.

Often you will hear people say that judging is political. Certainly there have been cases of this, but they are rare. The reason we see so little of it is because the dog's work is there for ALL to see in a trial. If a judge puts up a poor worker, that had his sheep all over the field, over a dog that worked well and held his sheep in perfect control, he will be made a laughingstock. The judge is not the only one watching and judging those dogs and the majority of judges are well aware of this.

In some North American trials, the judge will believe that anything that happens (or doesn't happen) is the result of the dog acting or not acting. In other words, your dog gets the credit and blame for *anything* those sheep do. In order for a rerun to be granted the sheep must be obviously unsound.

The system of judging is quite sophisticated, with half points being deducted for minor infractions. In the higher level trials, scoring can get even more exact. Because of the nature of this system (which favors Border Collies), rarely are other breeds seen at these trials, though that is slowly changing. An all-breed person may have to overcome some local breed chauvinism to compete.

A.S.C.A. trials, on the other hand, are rather loosely judged (some say that is one of their faults) and many allowances can be made for the stock. However, because of the simplicity of the course, and the more open-minded attitude on the part of most A.S.C.A affiliates, there is much more all-breed activity at these trials, and a "rare" breed is more apt to place well at this type of trial.

Most local sheepdog clubs are open to all comers, and many are attended by local shepherds. The judging may be informal (with dog handlers judging in groups with scores averaged) and "rare" sheepdogs are seen fairly often, especially in some parts of the West. The most common breeds seen are still Border Collies and Kelpies, with an occasional Aussie, Beardie or other unusual trial dog.

HOW TO GET YOUR DOG READY FOR TRIALS

If you were going to become an Olympic swimmer, you would quickly realize that training to reach this goal is a monumental task. You would learn that the dream of a gold medal will require much time, specialized training, a great deal of preparatory local competition prior to large meets, and conditioning of your body and mind for the stresses and challenges that await you.

A trial dog is the Olympic athlete of the herding canines. It is very important that you realize that a trial dog is subject to the same pressures as a human athlete, and needs the same kind of conditioning, training and preparation, often including a special diet, to help his body cope with the stress of travel and excitement of trials. Many people marvel at and fully understand the Olympic human athlete's sacrifice, yet scoff at the idea of an animal requiring many of the same things for his training and mental health. Trial dogs, race horses, and other athletic animals need all the help they can get.

Trials involve travel, constant change, pressure to perform well, often inclement weather, and many strange people close at hand. Many wonderful working dogs never make it as a trial dog because they just can't take the stress.

The profile of the best candidate for a trial dog is a dog that loves new people, that loves to travel (no carsickness and *never* restless in the car), that eats well in a variety of environments (and eats *everything* in his bowl), that has no "touchy intestinal" problems with strange water or food, that loves to work new stock in new situations and does it well, and whose working ability and obedience even under new stressful working situations is infallible. I might also add that a good trial dog must be briming with self-confidence, especially since you sometimes get the most rank, renegade stock at trials.

Your first trials should be considered mere "training ground" and you should plan to lose them ... and lose gracefully. My suggestion is to start with a few local trials: You won't have to travel as far or spend as much money on the travel, your dog won't be as upset, and when your dog loses you won't feel as bad if you are in comfortable, friendly company with handlers eager and helpful to give advice and share experiences of their own "bloopers." Go into these trials with the attitude that you are there to learn what you need to work on, and to gradually accustom your dog to the new atmosphere. No matter how he acts, he will be somewhat taken aback by the new challenges.

I am not trying to scare you or be a "prophet of doom," but all too often a novice daydreams of going to his first trial and winning

Imp. Bullenbong Bulli, C.D.X., owned by Gail Ross, taking sheep down the A.S.C.A. course center chute.

all the "gold," being admired and envied by all the others there. The truth is, it rarely happens that way. Most handlers go to many trials, learning and refining with their dogs, and success comes only after "paying their dues" in more ways than one.

When you decide to enter a trial, your preparation intensifies. Don't plan to get your dog ready a week before the trial; start your preparations months before, and slowly work up to your goal. To prepare your dog's body to endure the extra stress at the trial, work him for gradually longer periods, always quitting before he gets fully tired. NEVER work the dog to the point of exhaustion and use "interval training" (i.e., conditioning the dog's body as you would a human athlete's).

The most important element, however, is your dog's mental adjustment. To help him, you must CONDITION HIM TO WORKING VARIED LIVESTOCK IN VARIED PLACES. Work on the ranches of your friends, or haul your stock to different areas, a new one each time. Expose the dog to differant terrain, wild, aggressive, very flightly or pliable stock, each by turn, so he is able to meet any type of situation. Try to find out what kind of stock will be used in the trial—but don't count on it as being that way for sure. If you are told they will have nice yearling whiteface ewes well dog-broken, that's fine, but still give your dog experience on wild, fast sheep, and also on some that will stand and challenge.

This process of working the dog in new areas on new stock should start *months* before the trial. A good schedule is four times a week work at home, three times in three different places. Another good thing to do to condition your dog is to have many people around when you work him. Set friends along the fence and have them loudly talk and applaud, play a loud radio, etc. If you are going onto a small course where the judge may be standing out there with you, get friends to stand out in the field with you—even use them for "gates." Place one person on the left about twenty feet away, another person on the right, and see if your dog can drive his sheep through them just like he would a gate.

One thing I have found to help a dog's concentration in duck classes is to use a "milling crowd." Have several helpers walk around (milling) while you have your dog take the ducks around them like panels. The fact that the people are moving (make sure they stay enough apart to let the ducks through) is really a challenge, and lots of fun. Children especially love to be the ''milling crowd.''

Another vital piece of advice is to OVER PREPARE. If the course outrun is 200 yards, get your dog doing 300 or 350 yards really well. Don't train for 150 yards and count on your dog going the rest of the way well ... he won't. If your dog is driving only so-so, don't expect him to drive well at a trial, don't *hope* he'll get by. Count on about 50 percent of your dog's performance at home when you get to the trial. (Perfect obedience at home often translates into barely obedience at the trial.)

Practice your handling. Practice particularly anything that will help your depth perception. This is especially true if the course is a big one.

Moving sheep through a trial gate. Watching the heads of the stock tells you where they are going!

Heading for the second panel, trials winner Moss Rogue.

You may have noted I do not encourage you to practice extensively over a trials course. I think a lot of harm can be done by practicing strictly on a course—it sours the dog and bores him, and certainly doesn't prepare him for a new place with new stock. I like to use natural obstacles (trees, bushes, shed, poles, etc.) for most of my practices, and only occasionally do I take the dog over a real, trial course.

A word of caution—DON'T enter a dog in trials before he is really well trained. Taking a half-trained dog into a trial is a certain way to embarrass yourself, and teach your dog that trials are a good place to "goof off." This is usually the beginning of a "trial wise" dog—one that works great at home but goes bananas at every trial, since he knows his handler won't correct him there. I know it is common for many Aussie handlers to take barely started dogs into trials, but these dogs only place in very poor competition. That's why a good, trained Border Collie wins at Aussie trials—it's usually because they ARE trained, and therefore better able to cope. An Aussie could do the same, given the right preparation. If you are competing with a "rare" herder, have some pride and don't take your dog in a trial until he's trained and doing well. Often your whole breed will be judged by your dog's performance!

Trials are even held for ducks - with gaits in miniature. They are extremely popular with the spectators.

13

How to Find a Working Prospect

The biggest problem for the novice is where to look to find the right sort of breeders. If you already have a particular breed in mind, the first place to start is with that breed's own breed Club. Some of these clubs (North American Sheepdog Society for Border Collies, the Australian Shepherd Club of America, the Bearded Collie Club of America, the Australian Cattle Dog Club of America, the American Belgian Tervuren Club) have, at this writing, herding programs and award herding titles to dogs. Contact the club and ask for a list of breeders of certified workers in the area where you live. BE SURE the dogs are *certified workers* with whatever title the club gives out. Make sure both parents are workers, and get a guarantee, in writing, from the breeder.

Working dog journals, magazines and sheep and livestock publications are also excellent resources. Don't think you may not find any of your chosen breed; you will probably be surprised to find ads offering all kinds of herding dogs for sale. I well recall looking for my first Border Collie so many years ago. I looked at dog shows, with vets, in "doggie" magazines, but no Border Collies. Finally I discovered that I was looking in the wrong places for a true working dog. Ultimately I found that there were dozens of breeders right in my town, but they all advertised in sheep magazines and took their dogs to livestock fairs, not dog shows. Many of the AKC breeders who work their dogs also advertise in working or livestock publications, since that readership is more apt to buy their dogs.

Check the magazines and clubs listed in the appendices for advertisements by breeders.

If the breed you want can't be located this way, put the word out on the "doggie hotline" with breeders of your favorites that you are looking for a pup. Keep in mind that some breeders will try to sell you whatever they have and tell you that "all of this breed works"—don't you believe it. If a breeder can't, or won't, help you find *working* specimens of your breed, be persistent and try other breeders. Don't be tempted into thinking that if a dog is successful in another field (i.e., obedience), that it follows that it will also be a good herder. Though obedience training certainly indicates a high trainability, it is not an indicator of *herding instinct*, so do not take credentials in another field as indicators of herding ability.

All-breed stockdog clubs can also be a great source of working breeds, especially AKC breeds being worked by their owners for fun. Obedience clubs are apt to know about such clubs in your area, or contact those in your area who usually work their dogs (Border Collie and Aussie owners most likely) for such information.

If this all sounds like a lot of trouble, just remember that it will be worth it for your future to get a pup that will really work naturally. A dog is a major investment these days, and you will have the dog for about ten years or more. So a month of letter-writing is not too much trouble for your future satisfaction.

Once your have located a suitable litter, you need only decide which one you want. Avoid shy pups, and any that seem hyper-aggressive (rare in the herding breeds). Keep in mind, though, that pups at play do not always show all of their personality. If you want an AKC breed, you must also decide if you want a show dog that will work, or a pet that will work. Many owners like the idea of a dual purpose dog, although selecting a show quality dog does restrict your choices in a litter.

Chuck Eklof's Belgian Sheepdog at work.

There are many articles written about puppy testing, and many obedience enthusiasts place great store by these tests. I am not a big supporter of such tests, mainly because I've *never* found them to be accurate indicators of a pup's future herding ability or even of his personality. Also, I have seen too many people get burned choosing pups this way. One girl I know tested a whole litter and selected the ''best'' pup by virtue of its scores on the test—it later turned out she picked the *only* pup in that litter that had water on the brain and was grossly retarded!

I find that my own pups change radically from between three and five weeks, six and eight weeks, and undergo huge changes in personality at three months. Environment plays too great a factor. With my last litter a woman came out, wanting to test the litter, so I let her. I knew these pups through and through, having raised them by hand from an early age, and I knew which were dominant, submissive, etc., but I said nothing. According to her tests, the pup I knew to be the most submissive scored the highest (it simply had a good day that day). I knew this pup, and I also knew that my most dominant male pup didn't come off as very dominant on the test. The resultant personalities of these pups? The dominant male (who didn't test out as such) is still highly dominant, leading even the older dogs in my yard and requiring a firm hand to control him. If I had placed much stock in the tests, he could have ended up in a home where the people were prepared for a mild dog. The submissive bitch pup I placed in a very active family with four children (all over the age of seven) and she came out of her shell through tremendous socialization. When placing her I told her new owners to treat her gently, but even so she still cannot take even light corrections without screaming and running off. Had I relied on her test results, I could have sold her to a home where they might have come down pretty hard on her and been generally disappointed in her.

The point of this example is to trust your breeder as to the temperament of the individual pups. No one knows the pups as well as this dedicated person who has fed, cleaned up after, and spent many, many hundreds of hours observing and caring for those pups. When I buy a pup I choose a reputable breeder, describe the temperament that I want, and then leave it to the breeder to choose the right pup. I have never been dissatisfied with this method. You must choose an *honest* person, though, (I think the vast majority of breeders are, or they would't stay in business). If you are not sure, ask the breeder for references. The reputable breeders have been around a long time, and can give you excellent references.

Always make sure the dam and sire of any pup you buy are x-rayed clear of hip dysplasia, and certified cleared of eye defects by a veterinary ophthamologist. *Don't accept any less.* Some breeders are very lax about this. Make sure your pup is also guaranteed *in writing* against eye and hip defects. Be extremely wary if someone says they

Harvest's Chulita of Fairoaks, O.T.D., is a three-legged Aussie, owned by Nick Davis, who earned her herding degrees after an accident that left her handicapped. Many dogs have so much desire to work that they become top workers in spite of the odds.

won't give you a guarantee. Don't ever accept a claim from a breeder that such guarantees are not necessary because "There are no defects in OUR line." If you don't x-ray hips and examine eyes, *of course* you won't know of any defects until things really get bad.

Once you have him, raise your pup to be a member of the family and take him everywhere to socialize him. I never recommend formal obedience training (especially training to "heel" on or off lead) until *after* the stockdog training has progressed past the "outrun" stage. It seems to make dogs less inhibited if they haven't been taught to stay near you and watch you when that collar goes on.

As covered before, a young puppy should NOT be allowed in with stock *for any reason*. Should he get in, simply go to him, pick him up, and carry him away. Don't give him the idea that it is bad, and don't scold him; just take him away. He can, however, be taken to places where dogs are working and be allowed to watch (i.e., when you are working an older dog, at herding trials, at herding club functions, etc.). Teach him to be clean in the house and to walk on a lead, and the "Come" and "Down" training can start early.

Left to right: Rogue, Kamerer's Robin, Mann's Rogue, Jr., Pettey's Meg, Bridge's Elles Belles, Maxwell's Brazen Little Raisin. Trials winners and placers sired by Border Collie stud Moss Rogue. Always select a pup from proven producers of working dogs.

BREEDING FOR WORKING ABILITY

Herding ability, with its many components, is inherited, just as the structure of the legs and temperament are inherited. Many breeders of show breeds spend hours agonizing over the right breeding to provide their pups with optimum conformation, but take working ability for granted.

Litters produced by the mating of a dam and sire that are *both* workers are more likely to inherit this quality than those where neither parent works, or only one parent works. Likewise, dogs can be "cross-faulted" for their working faults, to create better pups than either parent in the working field. Qualities such as amount of "eye," whether a dog works close or wide, amount of wearing, desire to pull wool, trainability on sheep and many other traits are all proven to be inherited. The major true herding breeds (that is, those breeds where work is the main criteria) have greatly improved themselves in the last 100 years due to wise breeders who sought to correct working faults in each mating. Thus, a bitch with good eye and trainability, but a desire to pull wool, could be bred to a stud dog with similar good qualities and no desire to pull wool (or the ability to sire pups with no such desire), and the percentage of wool-pulling pups can be decreased.

Extensive studies have been done to demonstrate working ability as a hereditary concern. Two books, one by Humphris and Warner (1934) and the other by Kelly (1949) discuss in detail the breeding of working dogs, and carefully scoring the dogs for certain aptitudes, they also used progeny testing. The latter book, *Sheepdogs*, is of special import as it deals with herding qualities in Border Collies and Kelpies.

Though not dealing with herding, but with another type of working aptitude, tests done and breeding programs established to provide good working guide dogs proved very successful. Pfaffenberger (1963) has a number of things to say on this, and by selection for working qualties and ignoring conformation or show ring factors, Guide Dogs for the Blind were able to raise their success rate of their dogs from nine to ninety percent in twelve years!

It has been theorized by scientists that working qualities are the result of many genes. Some studies have observed that "strong" eye in herding dogs appears to be dominant. Further record keeping and studies may one day prove or disprove this. It has also been theorized that in some breeds gathering or fetching style is also dominant, but this has been debated by some authorities who feel that the gathering instinct is the *only* herding instinct.

The most difficult factor in breeding for working ability is in knowing what you have and what must be improved, and then finding the right compliment that will produce what you want without sacrificing what you already have. In order to know what you have, you must *work* your dog, and develop him to the extent that his natural qualities, plus trainability, may be evaluated. Many dogs do not show their true abilities until after many exposures to livestock. The dog must be *objectively* evaluated, and then future breedings planned with an eye to compensating the dog's natural faults as a herder.

Finding the right dog to breed to is never easy. Among the highpowered herding breeds, especially the Border Collie, there are any number of dogs to choose from. Often these dogs do not produce the way they work, because they are, as trainers say, "man made." That is, their skills are the result of clever training, are not inherited and, therefore, are not available to pass on to their progeny. (Each year hundreds of novices pay high prices for pups from highly trained British imports, and a percent of these will work nothing like their parents, since their parents were the product of master trainers. On the other hand, many imports have added much to the overall quality of the breed if they were good producers and had an abundance of natural qualities to pass on.) Therefore, when seeking information on the natural abilities of a dog, it is of prime import that you not only look at the dog's own performance, but also examine his trainer's observations of him as a beginning dog, and especially take note of what his pups are like.

Among the less worked breeds it is more difficult to find working stock, with few breeders caring or including herding qualities in their programs. As breed clubs continue to award herding certificates for natural ability and herding championships for trained dogs, perhaps we will see herding take its rightful place as a consideration of utmost importance.

The fact that many breeds can still herd even after a hundred years of not being used as herders, is a testimonial to the shepherds who labored over centuries to create these breeds. This fact also gives credance to the theory that herding qualities are the result of many genes. Shepherds of old did not know genetic theory—they simply bred the best dog to the best dam over a period of years, upgrading each generation, until many of these marvelous breeds were firmly established.

Caren Caldwell and her exciting Shetland Sheepdog, A-Roble's Aaron Corrie O'Banner.

Dixie von Shafferhaus owned by David Shaffer circles the flock.

14

Common Problems and Their Solutions

PROBLEM: A dog that constantly looks back at its handler while working.

SOLUTION: Such dogs are usually the result of too much mechanical training. I have seen very "mechanically" oriented Aussie trainers take a strong-eyed Border Collie and turn it into a loose-eyed, handler-watcher—all by the training methods used. I've seen those same dogs brought around and begin to concentrate and show eye again by proper training techniques.

Never gesture, point, wave your arms, or point with your cane, as these all cause your dog to look back at you for these signals. Do not use a lot of body language as you work your dog. You may do this without being aware of it, so ask a friend to watch you working the dog to determine if this is a problem.

Some dogs are just hyper-dependent and these dogs don't even need hand signals or body language to make them look around—a loud training voice or commands given too frequently can distract them. Make your commands sound like "stage whispers," and give only a few with time between each one for your dog to obey before you give another. One of my students had this problem with his dogs (both at the start were strong-eyed). When he came to me I realized the problem immediately—the man was hard-of-hearing and had been giving the commands in a tone of voice *he* could hear, which to his dogs was shouting. He switched to a whistle (all deaf or hard-of-hearing handlers should use whistles right from the start, with commands based on *numbers* of whistles rather than sound) and his problems vanished.

PROBLEM: A dog that eats manure or grass as it works.

SOLUTION: If you are sure your dog doesn't have a vitamin deficiency, then the next place to look is to yourself. Manure and grass eating while working are symptoms of stress, and are an avoidance behavior. With most of these dogs, the more unhappy the handler gets, or the more nervous the handler feels, the more these dogs eat.

It is then up to the handler to determine how to make working more enjoyable for the dog. In my experience, one trait all the handlers of dogs with this problem seem to have is that they don't praise enough (in a happy voice), they tend to over-correct, and they are perfectionists. The more frustrated or unhappy they feel, the more their dog goes into his avoidance behavior.

The dog should NEVER be corrected for eating things, this only makes the problem worse. The handler's attitude of negativity, coupled with the dog's sensitivity to the handler's moods, is what starts the problem in the first place. The handler must concentrate on *praising more as the dog is working*, and placing less pressure for perfection on the dog. Training sessions should be geared to an easy, relaxed pace, and the handler must be careful to speak in happy, hushed tones, rarely using correction and never physically correcting. The handler must also use only those commands that are important, and avoid a rapid succession of commands.

We have had nearly one hundred percent success in solving this problem *if* the handler cooperates.

PROBLEM: A dog that refuses to walk up to the stock, either staying back and barking or lunging in and gripping for no reason.

SOLUTION: These types of dogs are displaying a lack of power, which may be hereditary, but is more often a lack of self-confidence.

The best solution is to build the dog's confidence, and one good way to do this is to teach the dog to grip. If the dog is not far enough along, he should be put on very free-moving stock until he is advanced enough in his training to be taught to grip.

PROBLEM: A dog that repeatedly sharp flanks, pulling wool as he does.

SOLUTION: Once wool-pulling becomes a confirmed habit, it's very, very had to break. However, *if caught very early*, one can

A dog "flanking sheep," a fault easily corrected by proper training with a cane in the beginning. Note how the sheep have started to run.

eradicate this bad fault. It is important that the dog never be allowed to pull wool without receiving a correction for it—don't correct one time and ignore it another. You must be consistent.

Set up a situation you know will try your dog's patience. You may want to make the working area a fairly small one this time, so you will be close to the dog. Carry in your back pocket a throw chain (a 6-inch piece of chain, such as a chain collar without the clasps), or a foot-long piece of regular rubber garden hose. Don't let the dog see these and *don't* threaten him with them at any time. When he dives in to pull wool, whip out the throw item and aim right back of his behind. I like the hose best since my aim is poor and there is little danger of hurting the dog, even if you should miss and clunk him on the head, but with the chain you MUST aim well or it could hurt your dog.

You may want to carry several pieces of throw item so you are not empty-handed if your dog tries pulling wool a second time. I like to accompany the throw with a sharp word or sound of displeasure. Eventually, when the dog hears this he will figure something is on its way, and give up his idea. At this point you don't need to actually *use* the throw item.

Try to catch the dog just as the idea occurs to him and he is starting to move in on the sheep. Watch your dog carefully; all dogs get a "look" as they start to contemplate gripping. Throwing something at him is more effective at this time than after he already has a hold of the sheep.

Note handler's faulty cane position (holding it in the air instead of tapping on the ground) that allows dog to cut in and flank too sharply.

Certain breeds, and certain lines within breeds, seem to more or less inherit the desire to pull wool. This is one reason breeders should make every effort to avoid doubling up on herding faults when they breed. I have seen dogs that were simply impossible to break of wool-pulling—such dogs come out of two maniac wool-puller parents. However, the prognosis for an average dog that tries to pull wool a few times and is corrected right from the start is excellent.

If you can't bring yourself to throw something, or your aim is really off, you may have to run the dog down. Leave a chain collar on him and let him drag a regular leather leash. When he catches the sheep, run at him and get the leash in both hands and give a sharp correction, back, then down. But I much prefer the throw item; it is more effective since the dog gets an *immediate* correction.

In addition, I would say that wool-pulling most often occurs because the handler has not taught the dog to stay back out wide in the first place. With such dogs, I like to take them out and start them over, as if they were young pups, and when they start working sheep I *make sure* they get out and stay out wide. This often requires some hustling on your part but you will quickly find the hustle to be worthwhile.

PROBLEM: A dog that refuses to stop.

SOLUTION: There are a variety of reasons for this problem. The most common is a handler who was too anxious to rush his dog into working, and who did not spend as much time as he/she should have in teaching the dog the stop in the first place. One way to determine if your dog is ready to go out on stock is to take him out someplace without the stock, get him playing and running hard after a ball, frisbee, or family member, and from a distance, command the dog to stop. If he doesn't hit the dirt as if he had been shot, he isn't ready.

If this is your problem, go back to the basics and teach the stop the long, hard way, and don't let the dog back on stock until he performs perfectly away from them.

Another reason dogs don't stop is if they dread the command because the handler has somehow made the dog think it is a punishment. The handler who *yells* the command, *doesn't* praise the dog, spends a lot of time stopping the dog for no reason, etc., can give his dog this impression. Another way to make a dog hate the stop is to drag him back to the place where he should have stopped. I don't know who first came up with this silly idea, but it has surely made many dogs recipients of the worst kind of mental cruelty. Dogs don't associate the way humans do, so the dog doesn't realize that he's being punished because he should have stopped "somewhere back there." All he knows is that his loved one is dragging him, often repeating "Down" with the correction, and jerking him backward but the dog doesn't know why. He only knows that "down" means being jerked, dragged and yelled at.

If the dog doesn't stop, and you are sure he understands and is just being obstinant about it, then plan to correct him immediately, but DON'T drag him back to the spot you wanted him to down. Correct him immediately, either by running to him, or using a foot-long piece of rubber garden hose and throwing it at his rump, and say NOTHING as you correct. Lavishly praise verbally when he *does* down.

Make sure that you are not trying to stop the dog in a place he's not yet ready for. To try to stop the dog out to the side when he wants to get all the way to the far side (the fetch position), is very hard with a beginning dog that is primarily working on instinct. Be sure that your commands are working with, and not against, the dog's natural instincts.

PROBLEM: A dog that doesn't go wide enough on its outrun.
SOLUTION: This is seen a lot in the naturally close-running breeds. Usually, the handler is taking things too fast. With an obsessively close-running dog, it may take as long as a year, working up foot by foot, to produce a good outrun.

Some of the breeds that haven't been bred for work for many years should not be compared to breeds such as the Border Collie, that have. Of course, a dog bred for work and *only* work will have an edge and the training will go faster, but that does not mean that if you show lots of patience, your dog can't do just as well. Just remember that it will take *longer* to achieve the perfect outrun.

Take the outrun training slowly and when your dog is going twenty feet perfectly, make his next outrun twenty-one to twenty-three feet, not half an acre. Also, you must realize that some of the bigger dogs are carrying much more size and bulk than the smaller, faster dogs, so they will be slower and less apt to take the long way around. If you are working one of these big breeds (i.e., Bouvier, large Collies, Briards) my advice to you is to get any excess weight and coat off that dog and keep him in very hard physical condition. This is complicated if you are showing in conformation, since some of the judges appear to want to see "herding" dogs hog-fat. But excess weight is unhealthy, has nothing to do with the standards of these breeds, and will slow your dog down tremendously.

PROBLEM: A dog that runs too close, despite your persistent efforts to get it to run wide.

SOLUTION: Most dogs with this problem were pushed extremely fast in the beginning, and should be dropped way back to running big circles like the ones you did during the first two weeks of training. In these early lessons, the dog is chased out by the handler's body and cane.

Unfortunately, there are a few very tough dogs who would run right over you, break your cane and knock you down. For these, you may wish to teach a mechanical "Get back." Do this in your yard, away from stock. Start the dog from a down, chase him backwards with your cane, repeating "back, back," and if the dog takes even a few steps back, *praise*. Work up to where you can chase the dog all the way back to a fenceline or quite a distance. Then while you stand in one spot keep having him run back in wide sweeps (he needn't walk straight backward). Then practice while playing, and eventually use it on the stock.

PROBLEM: A dog that refuses to stay in the drive position, but tries to always circle and bring the stock back.

SOLUTION: Such dogs have always been improperly started in their driving—*always*. The most common reasons for this problem are that the dog was trained to "fetch and drive" at the same time, was pushed into driving before he was fetching well, or was allowed to gather and bring back the sheep from right out of a drive.

The solution is to *back up in your training*. If your dog is not gathering well, go back and work on that until he does. Then, when you start to teach the drive again, do it right, *step by step*, and *never* combine the gather and drive. Always make them separate lessons within the lessons.

Usually handlers hate to take this advice. It gives them a feeling of real progress to start the drive and they hate to backtrack and return to the basics. But they must if the dog is ever to become a good driving dog. If the handler chooses not to do so, this problem will persist.

PROBLEM: A dog that quits while working.

SOLUTION: There are many reasons for this. First, check out the dog's health. Has he had hip X-rays; are his hips good? I've had several dogs through my classes that were dysplastic and most start to quit after awhile. They love to work but working causes them a great deal of pain. Also, there may be other major health problems— failing eyes, anemia, heartworms. I had a marvelous Bouvier in one class that was super keen to run, but started to slow down and quit after just a little exercise. Upon close examination, the vets found a serious case of heartworm, and even though the dog lived through the treatment, he will probably be too weak to work. So don't immediately blame your dog's temperament if he starts acting funny; look for a physical reason FIRST.

Some dogs quit because they are hyper-soft and any form of correction makes them afraid. Some of these dogs were abused in their early months, or were not socialized. Some simply can't take criticism; it reduces them to a bundle of nerves. Many dogs like this are owned by persons who are very strong and domineering who have trouble praising but no trouble correcting.

Dogs that are hyper-soft need lots of *constant* praise and reassurance and little or no correction. A gruff ''No'' may be the most you'll ever use. You need to build this dog's self-confidence and over a period of months or years, you will find that your praising has paid off—the dog will become more confident and bolder.

Often the handlers of soft dogs say, ''Why, I hardly ever correct my dog, what are you talking about?'' But a long, hard look at their handling style is all that's needed to see the problems. The handler usually exhibits a very terse attitude, nervousness, a desire for perfection, and inability to act like a ''cheerleader'' for the dog. The dog interprets any or all of these as signs that his handler is not pleased with him. Dogs, after all, are only dogs. They can't say—''Well, that's just my master's style, I'll live with it.'' They only know that their master seems displeased and they take the blame directly. Because we are the smarter creature in this training, the trainer must adapt to the dog's personality—the dog can't change his, he hasn't the intellectual capacity.

PROBLEM: A dog that barks as he works.

SOLUTION: There are many reasons a dog barks, and you must first determine *why* the dog is barking before you can stop it (that is, if you *should* stop it).

One of the more common reasons a dog barks is because that is part of his breed. Many breeds have lines within the breed that are barkers (i.e., Beardies and Kelpies) and for some breeds, barking is considered acceptable. Though Border Collie owners find barking repugnant, one must be careful not to accept what is the standard of working perfection *for Border Collies* as the norm for *all* breeds. If all breeds worked like Border Collies, they probably would *be* Border Collies, since Border Collies are defined by their work. Most European and Middle Eastern herding breeds are loose-eyed, and among the loose-eyed breeds there are higher percentages of barkers.

Barking can be useful for forcing sheep without doing harm to them, and should not be rejected out of hand. Some individual dogs bark to force and if they do not lack power they should probably be allowed to do so.

Barking becomes a problem when the dog who is normally silent begins to bark, as a sign of a lack of confidence, from nerves, or as an avoidance behavior. Then one must analyze why the barking occurs, and how to correct it. NEVER punish a dog for barking— far better to find out *why* the dog barks and then naturally eliminate the need to bark. To punish a dog for barking, especially if the dog barks from nerves or lack of confidence (the more common reasons) is to compound the problem.

If the dog barks from lack of confidence, and is far enough along, in his training, a possible solution would be to teach the dog to grip on command to build up self-confidence. If the dog barks from nervousness, it is wise to examine what you as the trainer have done to make the dog nervous. Are you a perfectionist? Are you over-critical of the dog? Do you correct but rarely praise? Does your dog bark after you have repeatedly corrected it in the working lesson? Observe carefully *when* your dog barks and what has transpired prior to the barking episode.

PROBLEM: A dog that aggressively heels the sheep, tearing up their legs.
SOLUTION: Some dogs do this if they have been started on cattle and *then* worked on sheep. It is always wiser to start your dog on sheep first, then go to cattle.

But the most common reason a dog aggressively heels sheep is that he's bred to. I well recall a clinic I did. A woman bought a dandy little Australian Cattle Dog with an excellent style *for the breed* and her friends had advised her to persist in correcting this dog for heeling the sheep. She had been following this advice for years to no avail … her dog continued to heel. My answer to her was that she had bought a cowdog, bred for heeling, and it was unfair to her dog to try to make it something it wasn't and never would be. Many lines of Aussies and other breeds are aggressive heelers and probably wouldn't make good sheepdogs even if they were trained for many years. I had a young Aussie bitch that was so aggressive she would cripple sheep—creeping up behind and heeling and holding on to the point that the sheep would be bloody and lame. To heel was her life's goal, and no amount of persuasion on my part could convince her otherwise. So I started her on some good-sized beef heifers and she stopped holding on as she heeled. After a little training on cattle I gave her to a Brangus cattle man who was satisfied with her work.

You can't turn an apple into a banana, and you can't take a dog bred as a highly aggressive cowdog and make it a soft, non-biting sheepdog without a lot of time, effort and unhappiness. My advice is to not even try. If you have a very aggressive heeler who loves to heel at every opportunity (even if it's a Border Collie) work the dog on cattle—not sheep.

If you have a dog that rarely heels (but when he does, he does so with gusto), and you want him to stop, you can treat the problem as if the dog were pulling wool and correct it the same way. (See question on wool-pulling in this chapter.)

PROBLEM: A dog that has been incorrectly started, perhaps has had one or several bad experiences associated with this bad training.

SOLUTION: To the person who has learned the hard way that there are some very incompetent trainers out there, the advice that one should be overwhelmingly careful in choosing your trainer comes too late. What this person wants to know is "What can I do about it *now*?" Before answering this question I will relate some "bad trainer" experiences:

I have worked with people whose dogs had broken legs. This was due to a "trainer" who advised them to put their dog's front legs through its collar, which they did and the dog fell into a ravine while working. I've worked with a couple of people who were counseled by another "trainer" to use an electric shock collar to make their dog stop. As a result their dogs wouldn't go *near* the stock anymore— classic examples of teaching the dog to associate the stock with electric

The "one-duck" method. Handler defines a circle with a cane around the duck and herself so the dog *must* circle.

shocks. These are extreme cases, but unfortunately, there are many others. The lady who punished her dog every time it stood up for itself against aggressive sheep, with the result that her dog ran from sheep constantly and couldn't move them. The man whose dog was so over-controlled that he could not do anything on his own with sheep.

All these dogs need one thing first—rest, and no work on stock for a good long time. Six months to one year of lay-off is ideal. Let the dog forget the bad experiences he's had, the habits he's formed. Of course, he never really will, but you can help them become more dim with time.

When you do start to work the dog again, take it very slowly, and work away from anything he might associate with the past. If he worked sheep, use ducks, in a very different area, or if he worked ducks, use sheep, in a place he's never been before. You see the point? If you were the one who made these errors in training, then take classes from a top trainer and learn the right things to do.

For dogs that have been turned off stock by shock collars (NEVER use these things as they can even be triggered by local C.B. radios and are very dangerous to use), we have had good results by laying the dog off for a long time, then bringing him back with stock other than what he was working when he got the shocks. Start over, right from the beginning, but proceed very slowly and use no corrections.

With these dogs you have to make the work sessions incredibly short, maybe five minutes at first. Such dogs are suffering from a classic case of "aversion therapy," the kind given people who want to stop smoking that associate cigarettes with something really unpleasant. Now once they had accomplished this negative association and wanted to teach you to enjoy smoking again, they surely wouldn't give you a handful of cigarettes and make you smoke them. They would reverse the procedure and start having you associate only good things with cigarettes and work you up slowly, just like people who start to smoke in the first place. This is what we do with dogs that have been "ruined," We teach them just a little and praise like crazy when they do anything at all. This might take many weeks; the shortest time I've reclaimed a dog was two weeks, but some will take up to five or six months to completely get over their experiences.

If your dog has been taught to be afraid of sheep, you must lay him up and then start over, using ducks at first, praising the dog all the time. Start as though the dog were a pup, and after he gets to the point where you can teach him to grip, switch from ducks to sheep. Since this was the original stock, be prepared for the fact that it will take you a very long time to get this dog to come up and grip. Reward him for any stance he takes against the sheep. (See chapter on teaching to grip.)

PROBLEM: A dog that is afraid of the cane.

SOLUTION: This is most often seen in dogs that have been struck with sticks, brooms, etc. Sometimes this ranges from stark terror to just a mild aversion to the cane. This problem can be solved if the owner will be very patient and follow the advice to the letter.

The first thing one must do is carry a cane around all the time. Whenever practical, carry it around the house and take it with you when you go outside. Lean on it, treat it as if it were a part of you. Day after day, week after week, your dog will see you with the cane and learn that it is a part of you. When the time comes to work your dog, carry the cane, but don't tap it, just hold it or touch it to the ground, but don't tap it at first.

One of the dogs we now own had been grossly abused with sticks and showed the utmost fear of the cane the first time he saw it (to the point of hiding and cringing behind a shed). I carried the cane around constantly, every day, and within a month he could abide the sight of it, but was still fearful if it moved toward him. In working him, I used my body more to get him out wide (walking toward the dog) and just touched the cane to the ground. He became a super working dog, and within the year could be touched by the cane and would allow me to tap it on the ground as well. He would even come up at the pen when I was waving the cane to help get sheep in.

Care must be taken *never* to accidently strike the dog with the cane. Also, it must never be waved in anything like an aggressive manner.

PROBLEM: A dog that is keen and trainable but has no defined "style."

SOLUTION: One sees this more in dogs that have not been bred for work. You have two options, teach the dog a style or don't work it. Some dogs are just too aggressive to teach a style and thus, may be hopeless. But for many, the option of teaching them a style works, provided the trainer is quick and knows what he/she wants.

There is surely a controversy over this. Ethically, should one teach a dog to have a style, then breed from it? I think that if you do teach your dog a style, you should at least have the dog spayed or neutered so the serious fault isn't passed on. Every year, many "man-made" dogs compete in trials, and some do quite well, but to sell pups from these dogs borders on deception to the buyers.

The most common way to teach a style is the "one duck" method. Take your dog, cane and one duck to a big open field. Place a clothesline or lead around the duck and hold the duck standing on the ground, but close to you. Have your cane in your other hand, in a position to slap it on the ground and make the dog run around you and the duck in a circle. Make the dog do big circles, and praise when he does. After about two weeks of this (when your dog is circling all the way around you and the duck every time), you can introduce two ducks on the leads, still holding the leads yourself. You may wish to move backwards at times now, letting the ducks walk forward to you and letting the dog come forward as in a "straight approach."

This training should be done over a period of weeks, to drill the circling into the dog's mind. When the dog is infallible with his circling and if enough time has gone by, you may introduce a third duck and turn all three ducks loose with no leads on them. Stay close over your ducks to be in a position to slap your cane and make the dog circle. When the dog is circling three very well, add two more ducks.

Keep the dog in the open for quite some time before doing any fence work. The dog can now be taught his left and right in the usual manner. Be sure to stand close enough to the ducks to keep the dog from zipping past and splitting them. Keep him circling. Working up to outruns is very slow and difficult, but with patience it can be done. Just remember to take it very slowly.

Most "man-made" dogs can do fairly well in trials, but in practical ranch work they are less trustworthy. Usually any time there is a serious need for the dog, where he must do some quick thinking or is under pressure, the dog reverts back to his natural "style" and chaos results. If you have a dog with no style and need a top ranch dog, get a better dog with a good *natural* style.

PROBLEM: A dog of six months or one year of age that acts very excited over livestock but when he is allowed to be with them shows no definite style.

SOLUTION: *If* the dog is very well bred, from top working parents, I would not worry unduly. Some dogs are truly late bloomers, and to try to force them to work before they are ready will wreck their natural potential. Probably the best dog I've owned never even looked at a sheep until he was fifteen-months-old. Some dogs do a "Jekyl/Hyde" change at a certain point.

You will note I make a distinction between a dog bred for work and one that's not. Though some duds do come from top working parents, the percentage is grossly low, compared to the poor dogs that can result from breeding for qualities other than work.

When someone has a dog as illustrated in this problem, and the dog is very well bred, I always suggest to them that they put the dog up for about six months and then try the dog again. Many of us are in much too big of a hurry, and try to get a dog running before he can really handle it. "Wait on Nature"—wait until the dog *shows you* he's one-hundred percent ready.

PROBLEM: A dog that works well at home but acts crazy at trials.

SOLUTION: There are a number of reasons for this problem; let's look at the more common ones. The first is not working the dog in various places on varied stock to prepare him for the trial. Used to a familiar area and stock, the dog is unprepared for what happens to him at trials.

Another reason for this problem is entering young dogs into trials before they are ready and well trained enough. The result is that they learn that trials are a bad experience, or else learn that they can run wild at trials and you can't stop them. There is such a thing as a "trial-wise" dog, one whose past has led him to know that trials are a fun way to blow off steam. Such dogs were nearly always taken to trials before they were really well-trained. At the trial, things got out of hand, and the dog formed an association that is hard to break. If you have one of these dogs, start setting up your own "mock trials." Invite your friends, and all the dogs you can find, and act as though a trial is in progress. When your dog acts crazy, correct him and repeatedly practice the parts of the routine that seem to set him off. Soon the dog won't know what *is* a trial and what *isn't*, and you are on the road to recovery. Of course, your dog must be well trained by now, or you run the risk of compounding the problem.

Another reason some dogs do poorly at trials while they work great at home is "trial anxiety." You've heard of "test anxiety" in humans, where a person dreads the stress and pressure of test-taking so much it is almost crippling? Dogs suffer the same thing over trials. Particularly vulnerable are the "strong, silent" types—the dogs that never act nervous and internalize their fear. Often they get carsick or have diarrhea when you aren't looking.

The effect of stress (new area, new stock, new people, many barking dogs, your own nervousness) is very hard on these dogs; they find the adjustment difficult. Some can learn to like trials, after many exposures and *if the handler* looks upon the situation as a chance to condition his dog, and is not so win-oriented that he makes the experience worse for his dog.

PROBLEM: A handler who falls apart at trials.

SOLUTION: This is the opposite of the previous problem. It is *normal* for novice handlers to be very nervous at their first trials. (In my own first trial I completely forgot all commands, my dog's name, my own name. Talk about embarrassing!) A dear friend of mine used to routinely cry before entering the arena with her dog. Another friend of mine would refuse his breakfast before the trial or he'd lose it (the breakfast, that is). For most of us, trials are like being on stage—some absolutely love it, but for some it's just plain "stage fright," but AFTER it's all over, you are so exhilarated that you can't wait to do it all over again!

The best way to overcome the problem of falling apart at trials is to enter every small trial you can and plan to go into them *just for the experience*, not with any fantasy of winning. With enough exposure, you will find that the handling becomes second nature (though I must admit, I still go to the handler's post with half-buckled knees). Once you start your run, however, you get to where you are concentrating so hard on the dog's performance that you lose all track of time.

If you are that rare person who simply can't cope with the anxiety of trials, you have two possible solutions: Let another person handle your dog, or learn to cope the hard way. The hard way means to get professional help in a class; get the instructor to give you a hard time and make you a bit nervous. A class situation is important since there will be other people watching (just like at a trial). Through enough practice, you will learn to _ignore_ your nerves while working your dog.

One final point—it really helps the nervous handler to have a top rate dog. Some exceptional dogs will look at their nervous handlers as if to say, "Well, Mom's zoned out, better do my best without her." THAT is the kind of dog that makes you feel great.

PROBLEM: A male dog who waters bushes and fence posts as he works.

SOLUTION: The more loose-eyed your male is, the more you will encounter this problem, especially if he's the "macho" type in the first place. Many trials have rules against taking dogs onto the course before the competition, but if it _is_ allowed, getting to the trial hours ahead of time and walking the dog in the area is helpful. Also, withhold water from the dog for one hour before his run, and for about twenty minutes to half-an-hour before his run, walk the heck out of him. What you're trying to do is make sure he's dry as a bone by the time you get called for your run.

If the dog persists in hiking his leg treat it the same as the distraction problem, following.

PROBLEM: A dog that is easily distracted and glances around, wanders away, or investigates things in the arena while he's supposed to be working.

SOLUTION: This is a truly embarrassing problem which usually occurs at trials where everyone sees it. The way to prepare for this is to teach the dog the word "Watch!" at home. Here's how:

Set up a situation in a small area where you can catch a sheep or duck, and then wait for the dog to become distracted. When he glances away (or whatever he does), tell him "Watch, watch!" and then catch a sheep or duck. When he comes up excitedly to see what's happening, release the animal and praise your dog. Soon, whenever you say "Watch!" in an excited voice, your dog will be right up on the stock, with his head pointed in the right direction since he doesn't want to miss out on the fun.

Eventually you can progress to just feinting as though to catch a sheep or duck, and finally you can simply use the words "Watch, watch!"

In a trial, when the dog starts to become distracted (you can see it in that first glance away from the stock), tell him "Watch!" and praise him when he comes up eagerly.

If all you've ever had were strong-eyed dogs who'd rather die than take their eyes off the stock for a second, this may seem like a strange problem. But for those with loose-eyed dogs it is very worrisome indeed.

PROBLEM: A dog that refuses to leave his handler.

SOLUTION: First you must understand *why* the dog is refusing to leave. Is it a new problem or an old one? This problem is always easy to solve but it is often hard to get the handler's cooperation which is absolutely necessary for the dog to improve.

One reason for this problem is that the dog is highly obedience-trained. This does not mean your dog has to be a top Utility dog before he has this problem, even some dogs in training for Novice exhibit it. These dogs have learned the obedience (especially the heeling) very well, and seeking to please their master, the dog looks at livestock as just another bizarre distraction his handler has set up to "test" his obedience. For this type of dog, all you can do is be patient and drive the stock around yourself, praising the dog for any move it makes towards the stock.

Some dogs that are in serious training for obedience championships, may, at some point, have to have a choice made about doing herding at the same time as obedience. The heavy emphasis on "watch *me*" in the obedience ring and its more mechanical approach can sometimes create a less-than-ideal herding dog. This is especially true if your dog tends to be the "soft" type.

Another reason a dog won't leave his owner's side could be that the *owner* displays fear to the dog. Perhaps the first time the dog saw stock, he rushed out and bit an animal. The owner then got upset and let the dog know in no uncertain terms how he/she felt about the situation, perhaps jerking the dog backward. Some dogs like this (the ones that are more sensitive to their masters) take their cue from this and figure they won't run after those beasts again, since their master got so upset the last time. Often the owners have a certain amount of fear about "letting the dog go" and as a result actually unconsciously encourage the dog to stay at their side. If the owners will change their attitude, the situation will improve.

Another reason could be that the dog had an early experience that made him frightened of stock. For instance, he may have rushed up to an old ewe that promptly plowed him into a fence. Such dogs need to be worked on some very free-moving stock that will build their confidence. Eventually they can be taught to grip. You may have to do a lot of driving the stock around yourself to get the dog to participate. It is always a possibility that some may never recover if the bad experience was in their youth (*Never try to work a pup*).

It is often my experience that this problem must be solved through the handler. The handler must do some "soul-searching" about what he/she really wants from this dog. Some decide they want only a top obedience dog, a High in Trial scorer, while others decide they want a herding dog who also does obedience. Some handlers learn to understand their dog better and let it work some on its own, while others never get over their fear that the dog can't be trusted. Some handlers are defensive about having worked their dog as a young pup, refusing to believe that any sort of negative experience to the dog could have lasting effects.

Once in awhile you see the problem appear all of a sudden where before the dog was running well. Nearly always this reflects some "trauma" that has recently occurred for the dog. It could be the death of someone the dog loved (or the family's reaction to the loss), it could be being punished for trying to "herd" a pet parrot, it could be any number of things. One must identify the trauma, and then eliminate it, if possible, while continuing to give the dog great encouragement in his work.

PROBLEM: A dog that goes too fast.

SOLUTION: This is almost exclusively a complaint of novices; rarely does one hear this complaint from experienced handlers. Those with experience know that a dog with speed is valuable, if he uses it at the right times. Very few young, eager dogs start out running slowly (unless they're extremely large dogs).

Where do we want speed? On the dog's outrunning, flanking (unless told otherwise), and anytime we ask him to do the work in a hurry. Most often when novices complain about this problem they mean:

  (a) the dog is outrunning them as he flanks, so they can't catch up, as in teaching the dog to run wide;
  (b) the dog is moving up too fast on his approach;
  (c) the dog does everything in high gear.

To solve (a) the handler must watch his own position more closely. Use a small flock that doesn't move too fast and DON'T chase the stock onto the dog. Walk *at the dog*, not around the stock as much. Force the dog out wide, so he is taking the long way around, while you are in closer to the stock. DON'T try to outrun your dog … you can't. Make him run so wide that you can *walk* around. Walk *at the dog*, not in a tight circle around the stock.

To solve (b) the handler must use the "stop" to slow the dog's approach. Each time the dog jumps up to run, set him down. Soon he will begin to anticipate, though it may take many weeks or even months of practice.

For the dog that does everything in high gear (c), many novices have a tendency to over-control at first. If their dog is speeding along, it gives them a feeling of powerlessness so they try to slow the dog down *all the time*. There is nothing wrong with a dog flanking fast *so long as he is wide enough*, and the novice should not attempt to slow a dog down until he is actually working on re-directs. If the sheep are moving too fast as the dog is flanking, then the dog is running too close. Don't attempt to control by always using the stop; you will end up with a mechanical dog that moves in a jerky manner.

PROBLEM: A dog that moves erratically or jerky on the stock.

SOLUTION: This is more often seen in dogs with loose-eye, but any dog can have a jerky or erratic style. Some dogs become that way after too much stopping without purpose, while others just have a naturally bouncier or jerkier style.

The key is to get the dog stopping on his feet. I like to teach the down and then, over months, let the dog "fudge" into a stand. I use a new command, "There," for the stand. This "standing stop" eliminates the jerkiness of the dog's transition from the down to standing—that popping up motion which can alarm the sheep. However, I always teach the dog the down first, just because it is very hard to get a young dog to stop without bringing him to a complete halt through a down command.

PROBLEM: A dog that only runs one way.

SOLUTION: There are a variety of opinions on this one, but I have had the best results running the dog more frequently to the side he *doesn't* like. I have heard of some trainers advising running the dog only to the side he *does* like but everyone I have ever known who actually tried this, had disastrous results, with the dog *completely* forgetting how to run to both sides.

One way to combat this problem from the start is to make sure you run the dog both ways an equal amount of times—two left, two right, etc. But some dogs hate to run one way or the other, and you must be firm with them. Make them run three times the way they dislike for every one way you run them their favorite way. Some dogs will try to cut in front of you to get to their favorite way. When this happens, use your cane and slap it hard on the ground to get your point across. If the dog cuts back as he's running (he starts out in the direction he dislikes but then cuts back fast to run the other way), you can chase him around by staying about level with his rear end and slapping the cane hard behind him as you walk forward around the stock.

Most dogs will show an initial preference, and once you see what that is, simply run them two turns their least favorite way to every turn their favorite way. A lot of dogs will do better outruns one way. Again, you need to run them over and over that way, concentrating on getting them out good and wide enough. A lot of dogs run nice and wide the way they like, but cut in close when running the opposite direction. So, you have to work extra hard on that side.

This one-way preference takes a long time to overcome. Count on six months to get the dog running well both ways—IF you work hard. I have trained a couple of Aussies who were almost impossible to get to run both ways. In a very extreme case, using the "one-duck" method has worked for me, but you have to be quick and very careful. Personally, my feeling is that if a dog is this difficult to get to run both directions he probably has additional style problems and may not be the sort of dog a novice can train out. You may need professional help. Most often novices have trouble keeping their cane in the right place at the right time to keep the dog from turning back on them or cutting in across the front.

CONCLUSION

It is, of course, trite to say that all dogs and handlers have problems. Nearly all problems can be solved if you have a good dog in the first place. Problem solving should take the form of asking oneself, "How has my dog become confused about what I want? Could *I* be giving him the wrong impression?"

Sometimes I run into a handler who simply doesn't like his dog. Maybe they have had too many problems in the past, or a top handler has made this person discouraged about his dog. If you don't really believe in your dog, you will never get the best performance from him. If you don't like him, don't work him, or, better yet, let someone have him who *will* like him. Some dogs and some people just don't get along. When this happens, it's no one's fault, but it *is* foolish to keep a dog you don't love or even like simply because you bought him and will now hold on to the bitter end. A dog that drives you crazy may be your friend's cup of tea. But don't give up on a dog that might be experiencing a problem you haven't seen before. Many Border Collie handlers, especially, work with only the finest dogs. A great thing, but in learning to train average dogs you also learn a great deal about adaptability. Though I personally keep what I like and feel are top dogs, most of my students have average dogs that they love and want to work with. They can't, or won't get another dog, just because their dog has some faults. Learning to work these dogs and help their handlers has made me a far better trainer, and I've learned there is no one formula that works on every dog.

Meet each problem as a new challenge and use your superior brain power to help your dog. Make the effort to see things as he perceives them, then try to help him see things the way you visualize them. Incidentally, visualization is a technique practiced by many top athletes, and sports psychologists spend much time with Olympic athletes to help them "visualize" their best performances. It works with you and your dog, too. Relax as you work the dog, and *picture in your mind* that dog doing the right things. Many handlers have overcome some very bad problems by focusing their attention on what's right instead of what's wrong.

No dog is untrainable, though I've met a few *handlers* who were. In all seriousness, though, have fun with your training, and don't take it so seriously that it becomes a source of unpleasantness in your life. Enjoy your dog, the outdoors, the livestock, and the total experience. Good luck.

Waiting their turn.

15

Training the Trainer

From my observations during the last several years giving training seminars across the country, it is safe to say that almost 100 percent of the dogs I saw were trainable, but that not all of the trainers were willing to learn. That is not to say they *couldn't* learn. Unfortunately, many trainers go through a dog or two every year, always looking for the right one, when in fact the trainers' own lack of flexibility often is the problem. I am referring, of course, to the novice or nonprofessional trainers who just can't seem to find a dog that suits them. There is something wrong with every dog.

Of course, there *is* always something wrong—there is no such thing as the perfect dog. In addition, what is perfect for one handler may drive another person crazy. A great trainer works with each non-perfect dog, developing the good traits while minimizing the less desirable ones.

The best qualities that a trainer can have are a knowledge of herself (with all of the faults virtues) and a clear, unbiased view of her dog's strengths and weaknesses. A positive attitude, reflecting love of the sport of dog training, and a deep affection for her dogs are crucial. Understanding what motivates a herding dog is also important. Patience, consistency, and a coherent training plan are marks of the successful sheepdog trainer.

TYPES OF TRAINERS

I see three types of trainers most frequently at my training seminars. The first, and by far the best, is the trainer who handles and trains consistently but *flexibly*. The dog is clearly taught right from wrong, is praised correctly, and is handled with loving care. If something is not working, the trainer is willing to examine where he (not the dog) has gone wrong. He views himself as the most intelligent part of the team, with the dog being a willing partner who wants to please but who occasionally is subject to confusion. This trainer does not use the dog as an outlet for stress, and the dog clearly loves to work and admires his "boss." This type of trainer will always rise to the top no matter what type of dog he is working.

The second type of trainer I call the FIRMLY ENTRENCHED. This trainer has been doing things the same way as long as he can remember. No amount of talking or showing will convince this person. He often seeks advice from more experienced trainers, but either doesn't find time to practice or discounts the advice given. He has a set mind about his dog—either the dog is *wonderful* and has no faults, or he is *awful* and can't do anything right. Often this trainer is engaged in a "war of wills" with the dog and has either a very demanding or very passive attitude toward the dog. He tends to see everything in black and white, and the dog reacts accordingly. At his worst, the dog behaves like the slave of a tyrant, or like the head wolf in a pack.

A third type of trainer commonly encountered is the SCATTERSHOT. This trainer is seen more frequently now that seminars and classes with famous sheepdog trainers are common. She is seen at all the seminars, but instead of taking only what might work with her own dog, she wholeheartedly adopts the entire training regimen of each new "expert." This can lead to a totally inconsistent approach to training. One week the dog is corrected for pulling wool, and the next week he is being praised and petted. Another time the dog is worked hard to "get back out" in an average-size lot, while the next week he is allowed to run close in a lounging ring! Both the trainer and the dog are highly confused, and the dog often stops trusting the trainer or is subject to needless mental abuse. This last type of trainer needs to gain the maturity and experience to trust her own instincts and to choose techniques based on a knowledge of her own dog. A good trainer will attend a clinic and learn a few new techniques that might work, based on a clear understanding of her dog (or if not her current dog, with another dog later on). The "star-struck" trainer does not know how to say "No" to a new training idea that may be great for some dogs, but not for her dog. This indecisiveness leads to a lack of a coherent training plan.

POSITIVE AND NEGATIVE RESPONSES

A trainer's attitude is reflected in the confidence and attitude of her dog. During one clinic, a very congenial lady brought a Border Collie that had been running out of control for a year. She had tried all that time, using one method, to control the dog, to no avail. When her dog entered the working area, this owner immediately began to recount a litany of terrible things that the dog had done. Her dog sat sullenly, staring at nothing. When I asked about the dog's good traits, the lady continued with a list of the horrors he had committed. When we turned the dog loose to work, the owner was right at my side, telling me mistakes that the dog had made in similar situations. Finally I asked her to simply be quiet and to enjoy the nice things that her dog was doing at the moment. This dog was nothing more than a victim of his owner's fears and negative attitude.

Another owner came to me with a dog that had terrorized a wide variety of trainers with its aggressive attitude. All of these trainers had used a very aggressive approach with the dog, who in turn had jumped on the sheep. I tried a different, gentler approach, and the dog responded within fifteen minutes. This was not a training miracle, only the result of using common sense. If one method is not working and hasn't for a long time, try another approach!

UNDERSTANDING A DOG'S MOTIVATION

Some problems in training come from misreading the dog's basic motivations. It is very important that trainers understand what motivates the herding dog. While some trainers understand the limits of a dog's simple reasoning ability, other trainers attribute highly imaginative motives to the dog that are far beyond a dog's reasoning power. Dogs are not motivated by desires to humiliate their trainer or to get even for some past discipline. The average herding dog is motivated simply by one or two of three basic desires, in addition to his attraction to livestock. While some dogs are clearly in one category or another, some dogs overlap all categories. The trainer who learns to discern the dog's motivation while the dog is behaving a certain way will have a definite advantage.

Some dogs are PRAISE MOTIVATED. This dog is rarely overtly aggressive and often takes time to become seriously interested in herding. She is sensitive to correction and criticism and needs lots of praise from her trainer. In the beginning, this dog works as much for praise as she does for the love of herding. Her actions are often tentative in the early stages. *Any* good move should be praised lavishly, although the praise need not be loud or extreme.

The CHASE-MOTIVATED dog loves to inspire movement in the livestock and may do so with style or with a lack of it. Some naturally wide-running, circling dogs are chase motivated. The term "chase motivation" does not refer to chasing style but to the love of instilling movement in the stock. This dog may or may not respond well to praise and correction. His biggest reward is simply being allowed to work. Do not spare praise with this dog, but understand that he wants to make things *move*.

Many dogs among breeds that were developed to herd cattle are BITE MOTIVATED. Some will turn off and refuse to work if they are prevented from biting the stock; for example, a well-bred heeler that is forced not to bite and that is always worked on ducks. These dogs, especially if they are a cowdog breed, often turn into chronic woolpullers on sheep. When working such a dog on cattle, it is important to allow him to heel occasionally to keep his interest. Some sheepdog breeds that are bite motivated can be conditioned to be praised motivated with the right handling. This is especially true if the dog frequently pulls wool.

Most dogs show some overlap, such as a chase-motivated dog that also can be motivated by praise or a bite-oriented dog that is also chase motivated. Keep in mind that this does *not* refer to a dog that has developed a bad attitude through poor handling, but to the basic raw material.

Misreading the dog's motivation will cause problems in training. For example, some dogs pull wool to be aggressive and predatory, while others do so from *fear of the stock*. A dog that consistently pulls wool when asked to go in between a fence and a band of sheep, for example, may be showing fear rather that aggression. Such a dog "gets one in first" to intimidate because she feels

Collie driving nicely during herding test.

powerless. I like to observe such dogs closely before deciding on a course of action. A sure clue with a dog like this is when you catch a sheep and walk toward this dog in a small area-the dog will back away and try to get out of the way of the sheep that is moving toward her. She may try to run away or circle around behind to grab hold of the sheep's flank. Such dogs often grab wool when sheep are running away from them but will not face a sheep head-to-head.

Knowing what motivates your dog can avert problems and make training progress more rapidly.

Handlers routinely attribute to their dogs motives and mental abilities that simply do not exist. Dogs do not think and reason like humans. While they exhibit amazing ability, they do not have *human* mental processes. Dogs have emotions like jealousy, anger, fear, and affection, but they do not have as wide a range of emotions as humans have, and they do not give meaning to their emotions. You can make a better comparison by thinking of the dog in about the same terms as a two-year-old human baby. The baby sees an object on the coffee table and reaches for it. You tell the baby "no" and take away the object. But if you explain a lot about the object, or scold the baby for his motives for touching the object, he will not be able to comprehend. In the same way, a dog sees a sheep and wants to make it move or wants to bite it. For you to assume that the dog wants to bite the sheep for complicated reasons like embarrassing you in front of your friends or to get back at you is attributing motivations to the dog that are way above his ability. A dog bites because it would feel or taste good to do so (predatory, bite motivated) or because it might make the sheep move (chase motivated), or simply because the dog is afraid (fear motivated).

Because adults give events meaning, they learn from those events to alter their behavior. A small child who is scolded for taking a cookie from the jar on Sunday will remember the scolding the next time she thinks about taking the cookie on Thursday. Dogs do not have the ability to give this kind of meaning to events. Handlers have said to me, "I give Spot a good yelling before a trial and he really works better. He knows what I am warning him about." The truth is Spot may pick up that Handler is in a foul mood, and this instills fear in the dog. This may trigger aggression or nervousness.

Some handlers beat the dog after a bad performance at a trial, thinking that the dog will recall the beating next time it tries to fool around during a trial. In the dog's reasoning process, however, he sees that he worked the sheep in a public place and was beaten for it. This is the only connection that the dog can make. A similar example is when a handler hits a dog when it returns home after running away earlier in the day. The dog cannot connect the punishment with what happened earlier in the day; instead, he connects the hitting with his coming home (the event preceding the blow).

The late Parcana Pay the Piper HC, owned by the author.

For correction (not beatings, which are always cruelty) to work, the correction must be identified clearly with the event you want to correct; in other words, administered either during the event or immediately following it. A dog can never be corrected in the present for something that happened in the past or that is yet to happen in the future! Handlers should always remember:

DOGS ARE <u>DETERRED</u>, BUT <u>NEVER MOTIVATED</u>,
BY PUNISHMENT.

DIFFERENTLY ABLED TRAINERS

In the last several years, there has been an enormous growth of interest in dog training among the differently abled. People in wheelchairs, or with some type of physical or mental disability, can really enjoy getting out with a wonderful dog in the same way that we all do. Many make really first-rate trainers and handlers, and I would love to see our trail courses designed in ways that would accommodate trainers in wheelchairs. Courses now are usually held in deep sand (such as in horse-show arenas) or in dense pastures (often muddy and deep) that make wheelchair access difficult or impossible. In addition, some of the course design itself is strictly for the able-bodied handlers—the gates to the pens at most trials are quite a challenge if you are in a wheelchair or do not have use of two limbs to open them.

Differently abled trainers should, I believe, try to work with the best dog that they can find. Usually they want to work with the dog that they already have, but if there is a choice, I would recommend one of the breeds that requires less stern correction. This does not mean that if you are differently abled and have a quiet, biddable Bouvier you should not work with him; however, a dog that is very strong-minded and tough and a trainer who is physically challenged in some way make a bad combination.

If you have a choice, select a bread such as a Sheltie, Collie, a Beardie, a Border Collie, or any breed that is eager to please and that corrects well by voice. If you are hearing impaired and want to use hand signals, select a breed that is loose eyed.

If you have a chance to work with a first-class trainer, do so. Working with a trainer at the beginning can help overcome some of the early problems. If your physical disabilities preclude physical correction of the dog (i.e., running it down, delivering a "down" correction, etc.), then the trainer can do this at first, making sure that the dog doesn't get the idea that he can do as he pleases.

A word to professional trainers with differently abled clients: it is a big temptation to take over all of the handler's responsibilities. DON'T! Discuss with the handler the nature of what he can and cannot do. *Let the handler decide* where you will be needed and where he can handle the training alone. Do not condescend, and try not to be over-protective! After all, the handler/trainer already knows that there are hazards in this training, especially from running sheep. And handlers—be assertive! If your trainer is doing too much for you, say something! Don't expect the trainer alone to design the course of training; give your input.

I generally suggest to the hearing impaired that they train immediately with whistles rather that with hand signals; however, they must decide for themselves what feels comfortable. For those used to communication with their hands (as in sign language), it just may feel more natural to use hand signals or to gesture with a cane or stick. If whistles are used, make their signals based on number and length of whistles, not on sound inflections.

If the handler has some type of mental disability where the left and right commands become confused (not that we ALL don't feel that way!), and this technique becomes too difficult, substitute a generic command such as "Get around." Some handlers have problems with the use of words or phrases and may do better with sounds. One handler I worked with used a clucking sound (like the "giddiup" sound you make to a horse) to move the dog forward, a hiss to stop it, and a smacking sound with the lips to send the dog around. He was a great handler! An injury in a car accident caused him to have trouble with commands but not with generic sounds. So you can see how important it is to talk over with the client just what feels comfortable and possible. It's very individual.

This section is not meant to be exhaustive. Those of us who are able-bodied trainers are learning more from our differently-abled clients than they are learning from us! We have a long way to go before we have learned all that we need to. Trainers suffer from the same prejudices and problems as the general public when it comes to dealing with physically and mentally challenged people. We need to remember to be more open and to not approach others through our biases.

CHILDREN AS TRAINERS

Children make great sheepdog handlers if given the right dog and if adults do not make the training experience unpleasant for them by expecting too much. A negative, demanding parent can rapidly kill a child's interest in training.

Above all, a child must have the right dog. A very young child needs a *started* dog of correct temperament. She can then learn to handle it and continue training up to a higher level. The older child can raise a pup and start it, but I suggest that a child work with a professional trainer—one who is accustomed to working with children and who gives a lot of positive feedback.

A very honest dog, easy to handle and easy to correct, is ideal for a child. A small child should have smaller dog that he can physically correct. Do not give a fifty-pound child an eighty-pound Catahoula. Remember—dogs get very headstrong when working stock!

Some children with whom I have worked had dogs that were so stubborn and badly bred they would make an adult professional trainer break down and weep. One child had a Border Collie with such a bad temperament that it would bite him whenever he tried to deliver any correction. He was able to stop that and other bad behaviors, but the classes were fare less enjoyable for this boy and for others because he had so much to overcome.

Children should work their own dogs, not those of the family. Do not take Dad's dog out in the field and expect it to work for little Sally. Instead, let Sally raise or choose her own dog, which no one else in the family should train.

TRIAL ADDICTION

In the last twenty years, we have learned more about human addictions than ever before. Addiction doesn't have to be to drugs or alcohol. People get addicted to almost anything—even dog shows or sheepdog trials. I have encountered this type of addict fairly frequently at seminars. They are difficult people to teach. When *everything* depends upon a dog's performance, the handler is bound to feel upset and often angry.

If you are addicted to an activity, you can make it your life. And you can make your life, and your dog's life, miserable—not to mention the effect on your family. You will not be fulfilled or happy as a trainer.

Sheepdog trial addiction can start when you feel the need of a boost. Maybe life has become boring; or you may be looking for a few "strokes." The thrill of the limelight and the excitement of trials can be heady. This is no problem most of the time, but there needs to be *balance* in your life. If the dogs are creating problems in you home life, if you family feels that the dogs are getting the attention that they would like to have, or if you find yourself taking losing too seriously, it may be time to take a long look at your priorities. Such obsessions can make people bitter, split up families, and most important from a trainer's standpoint, can place a burden on the dog to fulfill your human life—something no dog can do!

Ask yourself the following questions:

- Are most, if not all, of my friends people I know from dog activities?
- Are most of my vacations planned around dog shows or trials?
- Have my family or friends complained about having to attend so many dog activities?
- Do my family or friends feel that the dogs are more important to me than they are?
- Do I get very angry or upset at the judge or the "politics" when I lose?
- Have I physically corrected my dog strongly after he gave a bad performance?

Remember to keep it light. Make training and trials a happy, casual, and fun addition to an already fulfilling life, not your *only* means of fulfillment. Your dogs, family, and friends will all thank you.

This handler shows good use of the cane to block her Sheltie from running in too close at a herding test.

16

The AKC Herding Program

The AKC Herding Program was officially instituted in fall 1989 and began licensing clubs to hold events at which scores toward titles could be earned in January of 1990. It incorporates much that has been learned from a variety of trial systems in America and Europe. Bear in mind that the AKC will most likely revise the regulations several times over the next few years as refinements are made. You can write to the American Kennel Club, Performance Events Division, 51 Madsion Avenue, New York, NY 10010 for the most recent copy of *Regulation for Herding Tests and Herding Trials.*

A SUMMARY OF THE AKC HERDING PROGRAM

The American Kennel Club herding program is divided into two separate parts—Testing and Trials.

The Testing section offers two titles, the Herding Test Dog (HT) title and the Pre-Trial Tested Dog (PT) title. In order to receive an HT a dog must pass two basic instinct tests under two different Testers. The tests use the same format which has been in effect in the breed club programs for several years. Tests determine whether or not a dog has inherent herding ability and is trainable for herding.

The PT (or Pre-Trial Tested Dog title) is for dogs which have received some training and are able to herd a small group of livestock through a simple course. Again, two passes are required under two different Testers. The Pre-Trial tests bridge the gap between instinct tests and trials.

The preferred stock for tests, both Herding Tested Dog (HT) and Pretrial Tested Dog (PT), are well trained extremely docile sheep or ducks. There is no prerequisite for either title, so dogs with adequate training may enter PT tests without having to earn an HT title first. For dogs that earn the HT title and go on to acquire the PT title, the latter will supersede the HT on their pedigrees, and registration certificates.

Breed clubs will still be able to award their own HC titles to dogs which pass the first of the two required herding instinct tests.

Trials offer four titles, the Herding Started (HS), Herding Intermediate (HI), and Herding Excellent (HX), all of which are suffix titles. Upon earning an HX, a dog can then accumulate the necessary fifteen championship points for the Herding Championship (H.CH.), a prefix title. A dog which earns an H.CH. title is a truly proficient herding dog capable of controlling even the most difficult livestock in diverse situations.

In the trials, dogs must earn three qualifying scores with competition at each level under three different Judges in order to earn the title for that level. Trials may be run on a choice of prescribed courses, and the titles do not differentiate between the course or courses that the dog has competed on.

The A Course is a farm or ranch course and demonstrates the versatility of the all purpose herding dog.

The B Course is a modified International Stock Dog Society (Border Collie) Course and reflects the type of work done when sheep are kept free-roaming in hill country.

An Old English Sheepdog turns back two strays in a herding test.

The C Course is a modified European or Continental course and shows the style of herding used when sheep or cattle are confined on a small farm lot at night and taken daily from the farm to graze on an unfenced pasture.

Dogs may compete on any or all of the courses. Although ducks are permitted livestock in Started and Intermediate classes, the Advanced classes are limited to sheep or cattle (as are all classes in Course C). Permission may be granted for the use of other livestock in tests or trials when there are special circumstances.

The AKC program as, distinguished from other un-unified systems, provides three courses for trials and the varying divisions. Course A builds on what might be called the "Aussie Course," which utilizes many of the same principles as the course developed by the Australian Shepherd Club of America. The main philosophy is that the course must be able to be worked by both gathering (fetching) and driving dogs, because within the Aussie breed are all styles; also their trials are open to all breeds. Course B uses the principles of any good Border Collie course, including those of the North American Sheepdog Society and the International Sheepdog Society. Course C is borrowed from trial courses in Europe where the primary breed competing is the German Shepherd Dog, although other breeds also compete.

The variety of courses will prove useful, because so many breeds have differing styles and needs. Some potential problems may be that, once again, the sheepdogs are overemphasized while the needs of cowdogs are less promoted.

Concern is that with AKC approval owners will train strictly for the competition and will ignore the deeper need behind the sport. Of course, it can be argued that we already have developed "trial dogs" and that they are about as much like the average farm dog as Man O'War was to a farm pony!

HERDING TESTS

The Herding Instinct Tests are on the most basic level and are designed for dogs with no formal training on stock. The Preliminary Test requires no training. The second level, or Principal Test, requires that the dog must show five consecutive minutes of interest in herding livestock, must exhibit a controlled pause, must move the stock in short, straight lines with simple changes of direction, and must respond to a call to return to the handler (which may be repeated). A dog that receives two qualifying scores under two different testers will receive the Herding Tested (HT) title. A sample Herding Instinct Certification Testing Form, which is completed by the tester, is shown below.

AMERICAN HERDING BREED ASSOCIATION
HERDING INSTINCT
CERTIFICATION TESTING FORM

Dog # _____

Breed _____

Registered Name _____

Color _____ Sex _____ Registry & # _____

Sire _____ Dam _____

Birthdate _____ Breeder _____

Name of Owner _____

    Address _____

_____ Phone # _____

Sponsor of Test _____

Signature of Representative _____

Test Location _____

On the day of _____ , I, _____
did test this dog for herding instinct using:

    _____ Ducks   _____ Sheep   _____ Goats   _____ Cattle

This dog, on this day: PASSED _____
                       DID NOT PASS _____   (retesting recommended)

With regard to working style and characteristics, the following best describes this dog's herding instinct:

    STYLE: _____ shows gathering (fetching) instinct
                        _____ shows driving instinct
                        _____ shows no clear style preference

    APPROACH: _____ runs wide
                        _____ runs wide through training
                        _____ runs close

    WEARING: _____ shows "wearing" to keep herd grouped
                        _____ shows a little wearing
                        _____ shows no wearing

    BARK: _____ works silently
                        _____ force barks
                        _____ barks a good deal

    EYE: _____ shows strong eye
                        _____ medium eye
                      _____ loose eye

    AGGRESSIVENESS: _____ forceful without excessive aggression
                        _____ uses excessive force for the circumstances
                        _____ shows no force (appears weak)

    TEMPERAMENT: _____ appears readily adjusted
                        _____ easily distracted
                      _____ frightened of situation

    TESTER'S COMMENTS: _____

_____

Signature of Tester _____

A young Collie beginning to gather at her first herding test--an exciting moment for dog and owner!

The Pre-Trial Test requires some degree of training on stock. A dog does not need to first earn a Herding Instinct title. In the Pre-Trail Test, the dog must be off lead and must exhibit a controlled pause while the handler positions himself with the stock. The dog is sent to gather the stock, which are moved through panels in a serpentine route to the end of the arena. The dog is then required to pen the stock. Total time allowed to complete the course after the stock have begun moving is ten minutes. A dog must receive qualifying scores under two different testers to receive the Pre-Trial Tested (PT) title.

Neither the HT title nor the PT title are prerequisites to entering AKC herding trials.

The founding principle of herding tests was to stimulate interest in herding with an AKC breed. They were not meant to signify which dogs actually CAN herd (which comes with training). Neither were they designed to be money-making activities for the club, where dogs and owners are treated to an assembly-line approach without meaning to dog or owner. Originally, tests were not designed to be an end in themselves but as a jumping off point for owners to get started in herding. They were designed to indicate possible *interest* on the part of the dog, but not his herding ability. Above all, tests were meant to be educational events where one could watch a variety of dogs and learn from the tester's evaluation and knowledge of the breed. They also provided an opportunity to observe the reactions of a large number of dogs. There is a tendency, however, among the AKC breed clubs to perceive the HT or PT as an end in itself, indicative of the their dog's natural herding ability, and to turn tests into an endurance event by scheduling fifty dogs in one day with inadequate help, poor setups, and few amenities for the tester.

SPONSORING A HERDING TEST

Tests are the most primary beginning of herding interest in some dogs. Many dogs show interest only after several tests. For this reason, you may want to have a practice day where the entered dogs have a chance to see stock before the actual test. After all, the point is to stimulate the dogs' interest.

Herding tests, even as instituted by the AKC, are NO indicator of true herding ability and should never be construed as such. Nor should breeders advertise that their dogs can work based solely on the results of these tests. Testers can be wrong, and dogs can have good and bad days; in short, tests are never final.

FINDING THE RIGHT TESTER

Make a special effort to find the right tester. When a list of possibilities has been provided, one person should be assigned to call the potential testers and ask questions such as: How much testing experience do you have? How much with your particular breed? What opinions do you hold about the breed? What do you need to hold a test? Ask in-depth questions.

Ideally, the tester should have a background in your own breed; for example, Collie tests should have testers who own and work Collies. If you are not fortunate to find a tester of your own breed, then look for the one with the most experience. Beware, however, of instant experts. A person who has not trained a dog to high levels himself should not be testing. Check out the reputation of your tester. Some are known for scoring dogs far too easily, passing just about any dog. Obviously, the tester should have high ethics and should be fair and honest. You can learn which testers have been brought into question on such matters by asking the herding chairperson of your national breed club or someone who attends many tests.

If your club is holding its first test, a good place to start is by contacting your national breed club herding chairperson and asking for a recommendation. Also, call other clubs within your breed and ask about the tests that they have held. What worked? What would they never do again? Get input—you are not alone.

BASIC REQUIREMENTS

Following is a list of *basic* requirements for holding a well-organized test:

1. The test is planned down to the fine details, months before the event.
2. A well-fenced, level area is obtained for holding the test. It must have adequate water, shade, and holding areas for the sheep.
3. Sheep are obtained from a reliable source, and are healthy and dog-broke.
4. The club sponsoring the event has *at least ten* reliable, iron-clad promises of workers who will separate sheep, pen them, run errands, help the tester, and fill out paperwork. These people MUST be dependable.
5. A tester who is experienced and knowledgeable in your breed and who has endless patience is obtained.
6. One or two more reliable people are assigned as special helpers for the tester—from picking her up at the airport, getting her to breakfast and lunch, and helping with other needs. Ideally these people should *not* have dogs entered in the test, which would place a double demand on their time.

PRE-TRIAL ORGANIZATION

Dogs should be limited to no more than twenty per day. The handlers should be required to come early in the morning and should plan to stay all day. They must be equipped with note pads and pencils for taking notes on what the tester says about their breed. Instruct them to watch all the dogs and to listen to the tester's appraisals. They should not chat excessively while the tester is speaking.

If the area is large, the tester should be provided with a microphone. Other items that they will need are a chair, cool or warm drinks (depending on the weather), fresh water, shade or shelter from the elements, a small table, and help with handling the certification forms. Plan for breaks and regular meals.

WHO DOES WHAT AT A TEST?

Following is a bare-bones breakdown of the people you will need to hold a test and the tasks they will perform. These persons must be absolutely reliable, hopefully with previous experience or access to an experienced coordinator.

1 person to coordinate with the AKC and/or herding club and to handle all official paperwork prior to the test.

1 person to handle paperwork the day of the test, and to act as ring steward. This person will check in participants, check forms, and process entries, etc. (You may have a separate ring steward is desired.)

1 person assigned as the tester's helper. If there are more than one tester, a helper should be assigned to each one. This helper will pick up and deliver the testers to and from airports, transport them to the test, to restaurants, etc., bring supplies or food, and generally assist the testers as needed.

4 people assigned to the sheep. Person 1 coordinates sheep rental and transport, providing food and water, containers, etc. The other three people move and pen sheep during the test, separate groups and mark or hold them, and make sure that water buckets are filled and that sheep are fed, have shade, etc. Poor care of sheep is making it more difficult to rent for tests. *These four people should be physically fit and dressed for the weather.*

1 person to give out material on the breed, perhaps with bibliographies of books on the subject. This person will also coordinate with the tester to find out what format will used and he will explain this to each handler as he enters the area with his dog. This person will help handlers who have trouble catching or holding their dog and will make sure that there are no loose dogs, that there is no excessive barking, etc.

3 people who are reserved in case of illness or emergency. These people need to learn as many of the elements of the various jobs as possible so that they can take over at a moment's notice.

An Old English "heads" a testy ewe at a licensed herding test.

PURPOSES OF TESTS

Keeping in mind that one of the primary purposes of a test is education, plan some educational activities as part of the event. As mentioned above, material on the herding work and on the breed(s) should be provided. Ideally, a brief lecture by the tester will give the audience and participants basic information about the test and how dogs will be evaluated. Give the tester an opportunity to comment on each dog.

Contacts with local herding groups and trainers should be available for those interested. A test should not be an end in itself. Remember—education is defeated by an assembly-line approach.

A test that is well organized and run will encourage and stimulate interest in herding. Encourage handlers of dogs that fail to try again. Provide information on opportunities to practice. Some clubs show films or videos of previous tests. Owners should be able to learn about all of the possibilities available for their breed. A fully trained dog of their breed should work at lunch or breaks so that novices can have the opportunity to watch a good stockdog at work.

HUMANE MANAGEMENT

Treatment Of Stock

Abuse of stock is rampant at tests. This makes it difficult for many clubs to find good stock to run. Livestock should be treated with the same care that you would want your champion dog to have! Here are a few tips for those who have little or no contact with livestock outside of tests.

- Shade, water, and protection from the elements MUST be provided for *each group* of sheep or ducks.

- The animals should be broken into groups and penned separately. A well-trained dog and three well-trained handlers should do this.

- If holding pens are not available for each group, a markingcrayon for sheep or brightly colored ribbons may be used to distinguish the groups. However, separate holding areas cause less stress to the animals (less chasing to catch them).

- Water buckets must be checked after each run and filled if needed.

- Handlers who are unfamiliar with the procedures for catching and handling sheep or ducks should be given an advance drill from the owner of the stock. Do not be embarrassed to ask for training. The owner will be relieved that people care.

- Stock must always be handled gently and humanely. Do NOT allow stock handlers to kick, whip, or pull the wool or tail of any animal!

- Do NOT allow handlers to grab and carry ducks dangling by the neck or upside down by the legs. Gently scoop one hand under the breast, with the other hand coming over the back and wings. Gently! Enclose both hands around the wings and body, and lift. Fold the duck under your arm, supporting its breast with your free hand.

- Do not catch sheep by grabbing the wool, or by forcing the head backward (this can break its neck) or by the hind leg. Sheep should be caught by placing one hand on the neck from underneath the head while the other hand enfolds the sheep on the back of its haunches, beneath the tail. The sheep can then be walked forward by gently encouraging it and pushing on its haunches.

A first-aid kit should be on hand in case a dog bites an animal (or a handler). The sheep should be walked about the enclosure prior to the test, and any that appear lame or sick should be removed from the group and not used. The owner should have vaccinated sheep against shipping fever and trimmed their feet BEFORE the test, not the same day, because it causes too much stress.

Ducks likewise should have their wings clipped BEFORE the test to keep them from flying. If you are unsure about handling or treating stock, ask the owner to be there the day of the test.

If any animal seems exhausted or lies down during the test, it should be watched carefully for stress and removed if it does not recover promptly. Teach your stock handlers to be observant. For obvious reasons, always rent about five extra head above what you really need to cover for lame or sick ones.

Never abuse stock! If handlers think about how they would want a stranger to handle their favorite dog, they at least are thinking along humane lines. Some tests have been closed down by humane officers. Do not allow this to happen to your club.

CONSIDERATION FOR THE TESTER AND STAFF

Many clubs don't think ahead, and their tests are miserable for both tester and staff. Treat your tester with the same consideration you would your favorite conformation judge. I have worked some tests where there were so many dogs scheduled that I was on the run (quite literally) for fifteen to eighteen hours without stopping. By comparison, most of the club members are out of breath after fifteen minutes of working in the testing pen. I have also done tests where no shade, no cool drink, no breaks, no lunch, and no one to help set up or handle sheep were provided. I have had to haul out and separate sheep as well as chase down dogs, and score. Clubs run like this find themselves unable to get testers.

Another routine problem is that most clubs have a few members who can be counted on to work tirelessly, while others sit around and enjoy the fruit of this labor without offering to lift a hand. The club president or herding chairman needs to be present and make sure that those who signed up to work do so. At one test I remember, one of the stalwart workers pulled his back during a long day of hauling sheep around with very little assistance. He later dropped his club membership and gave up herding.

As a tester, I have learned to simply *stop the test if people or stock are being abused*. A test cannot go on without the tester. I explain that until four people volunteer to help, the test will be discontinued. Also, as a tester, if you have been hustling for two hours and no one has brought you so much as a cup of coffee, STOP the test. Make sure that it is understood that you cannot continue without a break and refreshment!

A Beardie and an Old English and their owners meet outside the arena while waiting to be tested.

17
Breed Differences by Nationality

Today, as never before, we are seeing breeds of herding dogs from many countries participating in herding. In some cases, these breeds haven't been used for their original purpose for a hundred years, and information on their uses from that long ago is scanty. Therefore, it becomes impossible in some cases to determine exactly how each breed was originally intended to work. As a tester, I feel we should be less concerned about what breeds did one hundred years ago than what they can do now. This is a very *American* viewpoint. American ranchers differ from their Australian counterparts, for example, by insisting that any dog they use be capable of many functions. You might say Americans believe that dogs, as well as people, should be well-rounded and capable of great versatility. American ranchers often have holdings as large as do the Australians, but Americans are far less inclined to keep numerous dogs, each one a specialist at certain functions.

For example, a rancher may have two dogs. Both dogs are expected to round up sheep, put them through dipping chutes, load them into trucks, sort (shed) sick sheep, and then go to a trail on Saturday. In Australia these jobs would more likely be done by several different dogs. Not only do Americans resist the expense of keeping several dogs for just a few functions, but it almost seems that we Americans have a particular temperament when it comes to our dogs. We value versatility. If you doubt it, take a look at a lot of the AKC herding breeds. Many are champions, herding certified, obedience titled, sometimes with schutzhund or herding trial or tracking titles to boot! We expect our herding dogs to *be able to do it all* and we most value the dogs that can do just about anything that needs to be done with sheep or cattle.

For this reason, many European and Australian breeds are in a position of having to prove themselves to American herders. They must be versatile and adaptable to American circumstances and temperament. If we look at the breeds most popular in the U.S. for herding, we can see that they meet these qualifications. The Australian Shepherd is a breed with many styles and techniques, and its primary selling point is its great versatility. The Aussie can work any kind of stock, and do any kind of job. The Border Collie also can do any kind of job with sheep and is a versatile cowdog. They are used for sheep and cattle in their home country, too. The Australian Cattle Dog, while primarily a cowdog, is still one of the most versatile cattle-herders in the world. The strains which have enjoyed success here are those that can do any type of work with cattle.

Many of the AKC breeds that are becoming re-involved in herding originated in Europe. Though European conditions are different from those in America, I have not found that farmers there are happy to settle for a mediocre dog with limited abilities. On the whole, their approach to training is a bit more mechanical, but their goals are the same—a dog that can do a job. In the case of some breeds, such as Belgians and Bouviers, we have little contemporary information on how the dogs were originally used, but much can be deduced from their working styles.

I urge anyone beginning in herding with their dog to train the dog to its fullest potential! Do not be waylaid by anyone's description of what your breed can or can't do! If your breed is "supposed" to be a certain kind of herder, don't take that as a literal fact. Train the dog to do anything it *can* do. In recent years we have seen people who claim that certain breeds are a limited kind of herder, and they actually punish dogs that show great potential to do more! Many versatile dogs have been discouraged from reaching their top potential. There is no reason that your dog, no matter what its breed, can't be trained to do any job it wants to do.

Following are more specifics about some particular breeds from other countries

THE EUROPEAN BREEDS

On the whole, these breeds are "loose-eyed" and more easily made "mechanical" if the wrong techniques are used. Some might argue that they are supposed to be mechanical, but I think we will find that Americans won't tolerate a very mechanical dog. We like to see dogs work with enthusiasm and natural ability, and we tend to dislike a "robot" dog. Robot dogs require more "handling." If we want a dog that does more work than we do, this is not acceptable. Mechanical or robot dogs always end up making the owner do as much work as they do. The herding dog is intended to be a labor saving device!

I have found that the European breeds are *highly* versatile and enthusiastic herders if you let them live up to their natural abilities. For example, all the Belgians—Tervuren, Sheepdogs and Malinois—make exceptional herders with the utmost versatility. My guess, based on their instinct, is that there is no limit as to what these dogs can do. They can gather and drive, shed, do outruns, work huge flocks or small homestead flocks. Many are excellent with cattle and will head and heel. They tend to be rather close running at first, but can be made to go wider. The males tend to build up more steam, and some of these breeds do tend to want to pull wool, but this can be easily stopped—especially if the dogs are not frustrated and are allowed to get out there and move. This does not mean they cannot specialize. I strong believe that these dogs, like the Australian Shepherd, have their greatest value in their ability to do any job, under any circumstance. Why settle for less?

The German Shepherd, Briard and Puli are all dogs that show great versatility in their work. I know dogs of this breed working sheep and cattle on ranches all over America. I have grouped them together, even though there are differences, because in so many ways their styles are similar.

The German Shepherd Dog has all the requirements to really make it in this country as a versatile herder. It is not only a valuable guard for flocks, but it can gather and drive with the best of them. I have seen some German Shepherds with natural outruns that would rival a trained Border Collie. Though bred for large, lowland (slow-moving) flocks, they adapt well to any size or type of sheep or cattle. They will head and heel cows, and some do well with hogs or poultry. Over the last ten years we have informally tested about three hundred German Shepherd Dogs and probably ninety-eight percent showed excellent instincts. This is true for both American and German lines. Most German Shepherds will immediately gather and circle the flock. The males tend to be more aggressive. About their third or fourth time working they may need some correction to keep them from flashing in and pulling wool. They are tremendously trainable and should not be promoted as dogs who can only "tend" or act as living fences. They are equal in talents to many of the top Border Collies and its a shame that so few GSD owners want to fully pursue extensive herding.

Briard and Pulik are seen less frequently in tests. Some really want to herd, while others show little interest. Some take several exposures to stock, so a lack of initial interest is no predictor of future talent. There are many natural gathers among these two breeds. Some run close, while others are very wide-working. The main difference seems to be the dog's physical condition. The more fit the dog, the wider it will run. Brairds are very trainable and easy to work. They can do just about any job. Puli are the same, but a shy temperament can inhibit the amount of training you can do. I know of Pulik working on cattle ranches in the U.S. that can head and heel with the best. Some owner find that Puli coats can be a problem in brushy or fox-tail filled areas. Trimming the dog obviously puts a damper on show careers.

I have trained several Pulik on sheep and kept them brushed rather and corded. During the fox-tail season I trimmed only the feet, and this worked well. Others let the dog cord. Do not let a trainer discourage you from working either of these breeds. They can be exceptional and very versatile workers.

THE BRITISH BREEDS

Of these, the Border Collie is the best known and written about, so my remarks will be brief. The Border Collie is one of the most versatile and useful of herding dogs, for any kind of stock. They catch on like wildfire with ranchers because they are trainable, easy to work, and can do just about any type of work with stock. Some find them less useful in bushy, mountainous terrain, or on very stubborn range cattle. Much depends on the dog's lineage.

The Old English Sheepdog is a very different kind of worker. They are loose-eyed, upstanding and bold as brass. Their chief drawback is too much coat and lack of hard physical condition. If you keep some of that coat off and work the dog until he's hard and muscular, you have a gem in a good Old English Sheepdog. This dog was bred for versatility in its early years, but not much emphasis was placed on herding in recent years. Some OES just won't work, or do so in a half-hearted manner, but the ones who will are tough and can work any kind of stock, any way you wish. They are NOT just driving dogs, but all-around gatherers, drivers, guards, and jack of all trades. Since my family is from Britain, I have had the opportunity to talk to old men who were, in their youth, "drover's boys" who helped the drovers collect stock and get them to the weekly auctions. All said that OES (who were shaved once a year along with the sheep) worked every type of stock, often in a mixed flock with sheep, cattle, geese and pigs! They had to gather out of pastures, drive down roads, wrestle pigs into trucks, and generally make themselves useful in every way. Some OES will drop back and seem content to follow the stock at first. After a few months of hard work, the dog muscles up and may show desire to gather. "Following" was not due to instinct, but to lack of condition. Without muscle no dog can outrun sheep.

If you have an OES or any other breed whose style is a bit unconventional, but that works well and doesn't injure the stock, let it go ahead and work that way. For example, some OES (especially males) will jump at and practically wrestle down belligerent rams. This comes as quite a shock to the sheep! But if the dog doesn't chew up the sheep, I would let it do so. I trained an OES that would be very gentle until a 300 lb. ram would challenge. Then this dog (who was as tall as the ram) would charge at the ram's face, wrap its legs around the rams head and literally throw it! Now this might not be acceptable at trials, but this dog was a good worker that used a grip to move sheep.

The Shetland Sheepdog breed has many differing temperaments and a variety of styles. Most want to gather, but a few drive naturally. A bold, fearless temperament is best. Not all Shelties have enough ability to get them to trials, but those that do can be super. Although more loose-eyed than Border Collies, Shelties can do great outruns and also drive and pen. While some are too soft to be commanding, others couldn't be inhibited by a train! If you have a really soft Sheltie, let it work without too much interference and a minimum of commands. Some Shelties are excellent farm dogs, and they may toughen up. The stronger-temperament dogs are the best bets for trials. I believe in teaching them to grip right from the start. They may need to work closer (after outrunning) than some larger breeds. If barking seems useful, I let them. I prefer a very tough Sheltie because sheep see them as easy targets and are more inclined to challenge. That's when you need a no-nonsense little dog that means business and can really surprise those sheep. I tested one 6-month-old Sheltie pup who was smaller than the very large ducks we use for the tests. When a mean drake grabbed that puppy by the ruff, he shook loose and jumped at that duck--he was really angry! That's what you need in a little dog.

The same is true of the Corgi. Though generally not as fast as the larger breeds (though there are exceptions), Corgis should not be limited by their size—only by their talents. Most Corgis want to heel, but many will head also. If they are too rough for the ducks, work them on sheep or calves. Calves will teach them not to nip too high. Corgis must be fit and in hard condition. Most are very biddable, but really want to chase and bite. I let them "heel" at the fetlock of a sheep or calf as a reward for good behavior. In other words, several downs and straight approaches, some wearing left and right, then they get to nip at the heel. Using a hissing sound to send them in keeps their interest high. I would NEVER work a Corgi and try to prevent it from heeling! This is as much an instinct with them as it is with Australian Cattle Dogs.

Collies are another breed that you need to select for boldness. Some Collies are too noisy, but others use their "noise and power" to good advantage. The key is—does it work. A lithe, fit Collie can do any kind of job, but some show dogs are too fat, too hairy, and too out of shape. This can be easily remedied, and maybe one day we'll see show judges placing a Collie who is in fit working condition. Collies are very easy to train and should be started gently. If the dog is noisy, let it bark at first. Most will bark less as they become more secure. If they show any inclination to pull wool, teach them to come right in and bite at the nose of the sheep. It sounds like a strange contradiction—teaching a nipping dog to bite—but a lot of Collies pull wool out of fear. They are afraid to face a sheep head on or go in next to a fence, so they take a "cheap shot" after the sheep has turned away or is running. I also watch their tails. Collies don't always work with low tails, but if you've got one that barks a lot and waves its tail in the air all the time, it is probably showing fear or flightiness. These dogs may get more serious with time, or they may need to learn to bite. Most Collies are natural gathering dogs, but a few want to drive. Don't be surprised if your driving Collie decides to gather after six months. Some take a long time to come fully into their work. They are a very fine-tuned, high-strung breed that requires a trainer who paces the training at a rate the dog can handle. Don't push, but don't allow a Collie to get bored, either.

If you have a breed not mentioned, or are working with a rare breed that has very little information in print about it you have to be attuned to your dog. Let the dog work to its fullest potential, and be skeptical of "authorities" who tell you your breed can do only one thing, or is limited in any way. Many of these breed haven't been worked in a hundred years. How can anyone predict what they can do? I have worked Beardies, Canaans, Bouviers, Beuceron, and other breeds that some trainers believed were limited. All made fine, exciting herders. Your dog might not win trials, but then again, it just might. You are the EXPERT on your dog, and your dog is an individual. It is only limited by how much you can teach it.

The high tail on this Collie shows inexperience and lack of confidence. As she gains more working experience she will develop more power and ability.

ABOUT THE AUTHOR

Mari Taggart has been a professional trainer of stockdogs for twenty years. She is the only trainer in America to have trained and titled four different breeds to herding championships or their equivalents. She served as the first Herding Chairperson for the Bearded Collie Club of America and developed the program that became the prototype of AKC breed club herding events. She judges trials held under national or local rules. Mari is best known, however, for her emphasis on all-breed training, and for training other trainers. A long list of her students have gone on to become noted trainers in their own right. She is the author of *HEELER POWER*, a book on training Australian Cattle Dogs.

Due to time constraints, Mari no longer trains dogs professionally, preferring to concentrate on judging and teaching seminars. Professionally she holds a master's degree in pastoral counseling and works in a counseling ministry.

The author with Beardies Parcana Pay the Piper HC, and H. Ch. Rogue's Hollow Tweed HC, and Border Collie Moss Rogue.

OTHER SOURCES OF INFORMATION

ASSOCIATIONS FOR HERDING DOGS

American Herding Breed Association
Linda C. Rorem, Secretary
1548 Victoria Way
Pacifica, CA 94044

North American Sheep Dog Society
Rossine Kirsh, Secretary
Route 3
McLeansboro, IL 62859

Mountains and Plains Stocksdog Association
Roger Culbreath
32485 Hwy. 37
Gill, CO 80624

North American Professional Stockdog Handlers Association
120 West 400 North
Springville, UT 84663

TriState Working Stock Dog Association
Mrs. Francis Raley, Secretary
Rt. 3, Box 632,
Bedford, PA 15522

REGISTRIES

The American Kennel Club
51 Madison Avenue
New York, NY 10010

Canadian Kennel Club
89 Skyway Avenue
Etobicoke, Ontario M9W 6R4
CANADA

Animal Research Foundation
Stodghill's ARF Registry
P. 0. Box 490
Quinlan, TX 75474

National Stock Dog Registry
P. 0. Box 402
Butler, IN 46721

North American Sheep Dog Society
Rissine Kirsch, Secretary
Route 3
McLeansboro, IL 62859

United Kennel Club
100 E. Kilgore Road
Kalamazoo, MI 49001

BREED CLUBS

Australian Cattle Dog Club of America
3388 Hwy. 99W
Corning, CA 96021

Australian Kelpie
Working Kelpies, Inc.
Cindy Vondette
Route 3, Box 243
Willard, MO 65781

Australian Shepherd Club of America
P. 0. Box 921
Warwick, NY 10990-0921

Bearded Collie Club of America
Patti Carmejoole
80 Union Ave.
Sudbury, MA 01776

American Bouvier des Flandres Club
Ellen Raper
1718 Trinity Rd.
Raleigh, NC 27607

American Belgian Malinois Club
Mary Janek
Rt. 1, Box 32A
Farmland, IN 47340

American Belgian Tervuren Club
Eileen Hudak
1905 W. Carriage Dr.
Santa Ana, CA 92704

Belgian Sheepdog Club of America
Geraldine B. Kimball
211 West Elm St.
Pembroke, MA 02359

American Border Collie Association
Patty Rogers, Secretary
Rt. 4, Box 255
Perkinston, MS 39573

Border Collie Club of America
Janet E. Larson
6 Pinecrest Lane
Durham, NH 03824

United States Border Collie Club
Rt. 1, Box 23B
White Post, VA 22663

Briard Club of America
Sue Erickson
P. 0. Box 3373
Mankato, MN 56002

Canaan Club of America
Box 555
Newcastle, OK 73065-0555

Cardigan Welsh Corgi Club of America
Bonnie Scherer
Route 3, Box 271-F 5
Sumter, SC 29154

Catahoula Leopard Dogs
Stodghills ARF Registry
P. 0. Box 490
Quinlan, TX 75474

National Association of Louisiana Catahoulas
P. 0. Box 1041
Denham Springs, LA 70727

Collie Club of America
Carmen Leonard
1119 So. Fleming Rd.
Woodstock, IL 60098

English Shepherd Club
1251 Stevens Ave.
Arbutus, MD 21227

National English Shepherd Club
P. 0. Box 402
Butler, IN 46721

German Shepherd Dog Club of America
Blanche Beisswenger
17 West Ivy Lane
Englewood, NJ 07631

Old English Sheepdog Club of America
Frances D. Methelis
275 Naughright Rd.
Long Valley, NJ 07853

Pembroke Welsh Corgi Club of America
Dr. John Vahaly
1608 Clearview Dr.
Louisville, KY 40222

Puli Club of America
Carolyn Nusbickel
8078 Goshen Road
Malvern, PA 19355

American Shetland Sheepdog Association
Gloria Cronin
2516 Country Club Dr.
Odessa, TX 79762

Rare Breed Kennel Club
P. 0. Box 1244
Baldwin Park, CA 91706

SUPPLIERS FOR HERDING EQUIPMENT

Premier 1
Box 89f
Washington, IA 52353
whistles, canes, etc.

Border Corner
212 Salem Dr.
Everman, TX 76140
books, whistles, gift items

The Dog House
Francis Raley
Rt. 1, Box *14A
Crawford, TX 86638
books, videos, crooks, supplies

MAGAZINES

American Herding Breed Assn. Newsletter
4404 South 173rd Street
Seattle, WA 98188

Aussie Times
Vicki Rand, Editor
94741 - 54th Street
Dowagiac, MI 49047

Australian Shepherd Quarterly
4401 Zephyr Street
Wheat Ridge, CO 80033

Countryside & Small Stock Journal
312 Portland Road
Waterloo, WI 53594

Country Living
224 West 57th Street
New York, NY 10019

Farm Journal
230 West Washington Square
Philadelphia, PA 19105

National Stock Dog Magazine
P. 0. Box 402
Butler, IN 46721-0402

National Wool Grower
6911 South Yosemite St.
Englewood, CO 80112-1414

The Northeastern Sheepdog Newsletter
Nancy Hayes, Editor
38 Highland Street
Hopedale, MA 01747
(trial dates, ads, etc.)

North American Cowdog
120 West 400 North
Springville, UT 84663

Sheep! Magazine
Route 1
Helenville, WI 53137

The Shepherd's Dogge
Woolgatherer Farm
75 Bear Hill Road
Merrimac, MA 01860
(Border Collies)

The Sheep Producer
Rt. 2, Box 131-A
Arlington, KY 42021

The Ranch Dog Trainer
Route 1, Box 21
Koshkonong, MO 65692

The Working Border Collie
14933 Kirkwood Road
Sidney, OH 45365

Working Sheepdog News
Glynora
Llanfair D. C.
Ruthin, Clwyd. LL15 2 SW
U. K.

If you enjoyed **Sheepdog Training, An All-Breed Approach,** your comments and/or suggestions would be appreciated.

If you would like a free catalog of our entire line of books, please write to the address below or call us at 1-800-777-7257.

Some additional titles you may be interested in reading are:

Sheltie Talk   McKinney & Rieseberg $26.95
All you ever wanted to know about Shetland Sheepdogs

Beardie Basics   Rieseberg & McKinney $24.95
Complete breed book on Bearded Collies

All About Aussies Jeanne Joy Hartnagle $24.95
Australian Shepherd care, training, breeding

The Total German Shepherd Dog   F. Lanting $34.95
History, genetics, training, breeding, showing, care

**201 Ways To Enjoy Your Dog - A Guide to
Organized Activities for Dog Lovers** E. Milon $18.95
Includes herding tests, trials, and other activies.
 Addresses, rules, how to get started, and more.

How to Raise A Puppy You Can Live With
Rutherford and Neil $9.95
Care, socialization, development and training from
birth to one year of age.

The Health of Your Dog   Bower & Youngs $24.95
Complete guide to physical functions of the dog,
diseases, diagnosis, and care.

Write to:
Alpine Publications
P. O. Box 7027
Loveland, CO 80537
or Call 303/667-2017 or 1-800-777-7257